Hans Kelsen
A New Science of Politics

PRACTICAL PHILOSOPHY

Herausgegeben von / Edited by

Heinrich Ganthaler • Neil Roughley
Peter Schaber • Herlinde Pauer-Studer

Band 6 / Volume 6

Hans Kelsen

A New Science of Politics

Hans Kelsen's Reply to Eric Voegelin's "New Science of Politics". A Contribution to the Critique of Ideology

Edited by Eckhart Arnold

ontos
verlag
Frankfurt • Lancaster

Bibliographic information published by Die Deutsche Bibliothek
Die Deutsche Bibliothek lists this publication in the Deutsche Nationalbibliographie; detailed bibliographic data is available in the Internet at http://dnb.ddb.de

North and South America by
Transaction Books
Rutgers University
Piscataway, NJ 08854-8042
trans@transactionpub.com

United Kingdom, Ire Iceland, Turkey, Malta, Portugal by
Gazelle Books Services Limited
White Cross Mills
Hightown
LANCASTER, LA1 4XS
sales@gazellebooks.co.uk

Die Herausgabe von Hans Kelsens Voegelin-Rezension „A New Science of Politics" in diesem Band erfolgt mit Zustimmung des Hans Kelsen-Insituts in Wien.

P.O. Box 15 41, D-63133 Heusenstamm
www.ontosverlag.com

ISBN 3-937202-50-1

2004

Printed on acid-free paper
ISO-Norm 970-6

Printed in Germany.

Inhaltsverzeichnis

Kapitel 1

Einleitung

1.1 Vorwort

Die in diesem Band erstmals veröffentlichte Schrift Hans Kelsens unter dem Titel „A New Science of Politics“ ist eine ausführliche und sehr kritische Auseinandersetzung mit Eric Voegelins „New Science of Politics“. Hans Kelsen hat diese Schrift bereits 1954, also unmittelbar nach dem Erscheinen von Voegelins Werk verfasst, ließ sie aber aus verschiedenen Gründen, auf die im Nachwort eingegangen wird, unveröffentlicht.

Eine Herausgabe dieser Schrift schien mir sinnvoll, um nicht zu sagen geboten, weil das neuerwachte Interesse, dessen sich Eric Voegelin in jüngster Zeit erfreut, sich zwar in einer immer umfangreicher werdenden Sekundärliteratur niederschlägt aber bisher noch wenig zu einer kritischen Auseinandersetzung mit Voegelin geführt hat. Es scheint, dass Voegelin von seinen Kritikern ignoriert wird, und von denen, die ihn nicht ignorieren, nur selten kritisiert wird. Eine Ausnahme bildet Hans Kelsen, der Voegelin mit seiner Rezension der „Neuen Wissenschaft der Politik“ eine eingehende Kritik auf hohem argumentativen Niveau gewidmet hat. Grund genug hatte er dazu, greift Voegelin in seiner „Neuen Wissenschaft der Politik“ doch nicht nur bestimmte wissenschaftliche und politische Positionen an, sondern das Projekt einer rationalen, wertfreien und weltanschauungsunabhängigen Gesellschaftswissenschaft überhaupt, also einer Art von Wissenschaft, die Hans Kelsen, der sich selbst als Positivist einordnete, zutiefst am Herzen lag.

Die ethisch-politische Frage, um die es in dieser Diskussion ebenfalls geht, ob eine von religiösen Ansprüchen befreite politische Ordnung möglich und wünschenswert ist, wurde in der Geistesgeschichte unter anderem Titel und von anderen Protagonisten freilich schon öfter durchgespielt, zum Beispiel in der Diskussion um Carl Schmitts „Politische Theologie“. Dennoch lohnt sich die Auseinandersetzung mit Voegelins Variante einer Politischen Theologie und ihren Kritikern. Denn zum einen hat Voegelin, der – anders als der ehemalige Nazi Carl Schmitt – nicht moralisch diskreditiert ist, eine, trotz autoritärer Züge, sehr viel demokratiefähigere Variante von Politischer Theologie entworfen, wie sie heutigen Sympathisanten mit diesem Konzept eher vertretbar erscheinen könnte. Zum anderen werden derartige Fragen im Grunde niemals gänzlich erledigt, und erst recht im interkulturellen Dialog ist zu erwarten, dass uns die religiöse Politikbegründung in Zukunft auch weiterhin begegnet.

Der Kommentar zur Diskussion zwischen Kelsen und Voegelin über Voegelins „Neue Wissenschaft der Politik" soll jedoch dem Nachwort vorbehalten bleiben. Hier möchte ich es nicht versäumen einigen Menschen zu danken, die auf verschiedene Weise dazu beigetragen haben, dass dieses Buch erscheinen konnte. An erster Stelle habe ich Professor Dietmar Herz von der Universität Erfurt zu danken. Professor Herz hat mich auf das Manuskript von Hans Kelsen aufmerksam gemacht und diese Veröffentlichung überhaupt erst angeregt. Weiterhin möchte ich Josephine Hage danken, die mir beim Korrekturlesen und Vergleichen des Textes mit der Manuskriptkopie geholfen hat. Danken möchte ich auch Professor Peter J. Opitz vom Eric Voegelin Archiv in München, der mir einige wertvolle Hinweise zu Eric Voegelins „Neuer Wissenschaft der Politik" und ihrer Entstehungsgeschichte gegeben hat. Professor Opitz vertritt zu Eric Voegelins „Neuer Wissenschaft der Politik" freilich eine ganz andere Meinung, als sie in Hans Kelsens Rezension und im Nachtwort zu diesem Band ausgedrückt ist. Für eine andere Lesart von Voegelins Text und all denjenigen, die tiefer in diese Materie eindringen wollen, empfehle ich daher Peter Opitz' Nachwort zur Neuausgabe von 2004 der „Neuen Wissenschaft der Politik" von Eric Veogelin. Schließlich möchte ich natürlich dem Hans Kelsen Insitut in Wien für die Genehmigung zur Veröffentlichung des Manuskripts danken.

Eckhart Arnold, Düsseldorf 2004

1.2 Zur Textgestalt

Das Manuskript von Hans Kelsens Voegelin-Rezension liegt in Form eines 125-seitigen Typoskripts mit handschriftlichen Korrekturen vor. Das Original des Manuskripts liegt im Hans Kelsen Insitut in Wien. Ein Kopie befindet sich im Eric Voegelin Archiv in München. Bei der Übtertragung des Manuskriptes wurde größter Wert auf Texttreue gelegt, d.h. der Text wurde bis auf die weiter unten aufgezählten wenigen Änderungen eins zu eins übertragen, wobei die handschriftlichen Streichungen und Korrekturen jedoch berücksichtigt wurden. Hervorhebungen im Text, die Kelsen stets durch Unterstreichungen markiert hat, wurden durch Kursivschrift wiedergegeben. Ansonsten wurden lediglich die Fußnoten im Text – abweichend vom Manuskript – mit einer durchgehenden Nummerierung versehen. Die Kapitelüberschriften und auch die Nummerierung der Teilkapitel wurden hingegen aus dem Manuskript übernommen.

Das Original des Textes wurde von Hans Kelsen in englischer Sprache verfasst. Auf eine Übersetzung ins Deutsche wurde verzichtet, da die Kenntnis des Englischen im deutschen Sprachraum so weit verbreitet ist, dass die Zugänglichkeit des Textes für deutschsprachige Leser dadurch kaum erschwert wird, während umgekehrt sehr viel mehr Leser den englischen Originaltext verstehen können als eine deutsche Übersetzung.

An folgenden Stellen wurden Änderungen am Text Kelsens vorgenommen. Die Notwendigkeit zu diesen Änderungen ergab sich daraus, dass das Manuskript an den entsprechenden Stellen unvollständig oder syntaktisch fehlerhaft war:

1. Auf Seite 15 wurde in Fußnote 12 das Wort „philosophy" zwischen „Aristotle's" und „justice" eingefügt. Im Manuskript ist das Wort „philosophy" ohne genaue Zuordnung am unteren Rand vermerkt.

2. Auf Seite 72 wurde der Text der Fußnote 187 durch einen Verweis auf die im Text erörterte Textstelle eines Buches von Hendrik Berkhof ersetzt, da aus dem sachlichen Zusammenhang heraus zu vermuten ist, dass Hans Kelsen an dieser Stelle auf Berkhof verweisen wollte. Im Manuskript ist diese Fußnote unvollständig und lautet „Cf *Supra*, p. ...".

3. Auf Seite 99 konnte die Position des Satzes „The split into two worlds is the result of the Russian revolution but was not at all the result of the "gnostic" Puritan revolution." nur aus dem Textzusammenhang ermittelt werden. Im Manuskript ist der Satz ohne genaue Angabe der Position einige Zeilen weiter unten nachträglich am Rand angebracht worden. Der Zusammenhang legt jedoch nahe, dass dieser Satz weiter oben eingefügt werden muss.

Kapitel 2

Hans Kelsen: A New Science of Politics

2.1 A Crusade against Positivism

It is an undeniable fact that the extraordinary progress science has achieved in modern times is, in the first place, the result of its emancipation from the bonds in which theology had held it during the Middle Ages. The principle of truthfully describing reality and explaining it on a strictly empirical basis, without having recourse to theology or any other metaphysical speculation, is called positivism. It is another fact that a positivistic social science is not in a position to justify an established social order as the realization of absolute values. For it can evaluate a social institution only as a means appropriate to achieve a presupposed end, but inappropriate if another end is presupposed. That is to say, it can evaluate a social institution only conditionally, or, what amounts to the same, it can attribute to it only a relative value, "value" – positive or negative – meaning the relationship of a means to an end. This is a relationship of cause and effect, and can be ascertained in a scientific way on the basis of human experience. Consequently, a positivistic social science cannot evaluate an end which is not itself a means for another end, but an ultimate end. It cannot evaluate a social institution unconditionally, or, what amounts to the same, it cannot attribute to it an absolute value. The absolute in general, and absolute values in particular, belong to a transcendental sphere which is beyond scientific experience, the field of theology and other metaphysical speculations. Hence scientific positivism goes hand in hand with relativism.

When the foundations of the established social order are shaken by wars and revolutionary movements and the need for an absolute, not merely relative, justification of that order becomes urgent, religion, and with religion theology and other metaphysical speculations are brought to the front of intellectual life and become ideological instruments of politics. In view of the great importance science assumes in modern society, the – always existing but in periods of social equilibrium repressed – tendency of using social science for the same purpose increases. And this tendency manifests itself in a passionate opposition against relativistic positivism and the attempt to bring science again under the sway of theology and other metaphysical speculations.

A characteristic and very serious symptom of this tendency is a recently published book which has created widespread comment: Eric Voegelin's The New Science of Politics.[1] It undertakes not more and not less than a complete restoration of political science, which is necessary because – as Professor Voegelin asserts – this science has been destroyed by positivism. Voegelin does not underestimate the gigantic import of his enterprise. He says: "When science is as thoroughly ruined as it was around 1900, the mere recovery of theoretical craftsmanship is a considerable task, to say nothing of the amounts of materials that must be reworked in order to reconstruct the order of relevance in facts and problems."[2] In opposition to "destructive positivism" which shirked its task to "penetrate to a theoretical understanding of the source of order and its validity" that is, the idea of justice, the new science of politics is to be established with respect to this task on the basis of "metaphysical speculation and theological symbolization"; that is to say, placed under the spiritual authority of Plato and Thomas Aquinas, the main but not the only representatives of this type of thinking.[3] Voegelin accuses positivism of having destroyed science, but does not give any approximately clear definition of that school of thought against which he pleads his grave indictment. The collective term "positivism" in general, and the term "positivistic" social or political science in particular, comprises many different types of theoretical systems which have only a negative criterion in common: the refusal to have recourse to metaphysical – and that implies religious-theological – speculation. Voegelin seems to be conscious of this fact, for he speaks of "the variety of positivistic phenomena" and considers it inappropriate to define positivism "as the doctrine of this or that outstanding positivistic thinker."[4] Hence the decisive trend in his fight against positivism can be only the reaction against the anti-metaphysical attitude prevailing in modern social philosophy and science. The emancipation of political science from metaphysics and especially from theology does not go back as far in time as the emancipation of natural science. Until the end of the 18th century, theology kept political science under its strict control. The doctrine that the state is a divine institution and the ruler an authority ordained by God was almost generally accepted. Hence it is not exactly a "new" science

[1] Eric Voegelin, *The New Science of Politics.* An Introduction. Charles Walgreen Lectures. The University of Chicago Press, 1952.

[2] L.c., p. 23.

[3] L.c., p. 6.

[4] L.c., pp. 6f.

of politics at which Voegelin, according to the title of his book, is aiming. It is a very old one, which has been abandoned because it has been proved to be a pseudo-science, the instrument of definite political powers. Voegelin sets forth against positivism as a whole two arguments of a most general character. Both arguments can easily be rejected. The first is "the destruction worked by positivism", due to the assumption that the only scientific method – which, consequently, is to be applied also by the social sciences – is the "mathematizing" method successfully applied by the natural sciences. This argument is utterly wrong. For there is a school of thought of outspoken positivistic, that is anti-metaphysical and anti-theological, social science which expressly and emphatically distinguishes between the problems of the social sciences to which the methods of natural science may be applied with more or less modifications, and the problems to which a wholly different method must be applied. Since I consider myself as a typical representative of positivism, I may refer to my essay "Causality and Imputation"[5], in which I summarize the results of the methodological doctrine distinguishing between social sciences applying – as do the natural sciences – the principle of causality, such as sociology, and social sciences applying a totally different principle, that of imputation, social sciences dealing with norms, such as ethics and jurisprudence. These are the sciences which Voegelin has in mind when he accuses positivistic social science of destructive effects, the sciences dealing with the problem of right and wrong, of justice and injustice. There can be no doubt that a scholar of such extraordinary knowledge of literature is not unaware of this school of thought within positivistic social science.

The second argument set forth against positivism is in truth identical with the first one, in which it is implied. Positivism, Voegelin asserts, makes the use of a method the criterion of science, instead of measuring the adequacy of a method by its usefulness to the purpose of science. He does not make any attempt at proving this criticism by quoting writers guilty of this error. He reminds the destructive positivists of the truth that "different objects require different methods"[6] Voegelin certainly knows that nobody else has insisted on this truth, by stigmatizing the logical fallacy of "syncretism of methods", so energetically as the above mentioned positivist, whose main concern was, and still is, to show that the object of certain social sciences is totally different from that of the natural sciences, and that consequently a method other than the one applied by the latter is adequate to the former.[7]

But he does not stick very consistently to the principle the violation of

---

[5] *Ethics*, Vol. 61 (1950) pp. 1-11.

[6] L.c., p. 5.

[7] Cf. Hans Kelsen, "Was ist die Reine Rechtslehre." In: *Demokratie und Rechtsstaat.* Festschrift zum 60. Geburtstag von Prof. Z. Giacometti, Zuerich 1953, S. 147.

which he lays to the door of positivism: that different objects require different methods. He says – as an objection against positivism in social science – that if we are lead by positivistic social science, "to the notion that social order is motivated by will to power and fear, we know that we have lost the essence of the problem somewhere in the course of our inquiry – however valuable the results may be in clarifying other essential aspects of social order."[8] That a positivistic social science may have valuable results with respect to essential aspects of social order, is hardly compatible with its utterly "destructive" character. But it is not this inconsistency which counts in this connection. Voegelin asserts that by being led to the notion that social order is motivated by will to power and fear, we have lost the essence of the problem. Of which problem? The one he mentioned before, namely the question of "right and wrong, of justice and injustice": a question to which, as he suggests, we may find an adequate answer "in the Platonic Agathon, or the Aristotelian Nous, or the Stoic Logos, or the Thomistic *ratio aeterna*"[9] But this question concerns an object wholly different from the object of the quest on to which destructive positivism answers by referring to the "will to power and fear." The one is a problem of value and – as Voegelin's reference to Plato shows – the problem of the absolute value; the other a problem of facts, the motives of human behavior by which social orders are established, without regard to the question as to whether these orders do or do not correspond to the absolute value of justice. It is a positivistic school of social science that emphasizes the difference between those two problems, as Voegelin does know very well. For it is just this distinction which he later makes responsible for the destructive effect of positivistic science which insists on this distinction. It is therefore contrary to the principle according to which different objects require different methods, that Voegelin reproaches positivistic science for having lost its problem. The problem he has in mind is simply a problem different from that at which positivistic social science is directed by referring to the will to power and fear. Only by confusing the two problems, he can say, as an argument against positivism, that "the methods of a psychology of motivations are not adequate for the exploration of the problem"[10], namely, the problem of absolute justice, which is not the problem of the positivistic science against which he argues.

It is in particular for the solution of the problem of absolute justice that Voegelin undertakes his restoration of the social science, destroyed by positivism. What he suggests is in principle nothing but a return to the metaphysical and theological speculation of Plato, Aristotle and Thomas Aquinas.

[8]Voegelin, l.c., p. 6.
[9]L.c., p. 6.
[10]Ibid.

This is rather strange, for it is a "science" which Voegelin intends to restore and if the history of science shows anything, it is the fact that true science, as an objective cognition of reality independent from the wish and fear of the subject of cognition must be separated from metaphysical-theological speculation, that is to say, from the products of man's wishful or fearful imagination of a transcendental sphere lying beyond his sensual apperception controlled by his reason. If only that intellectual attitude had prevailed which is manifested in the metaphysical-theological speculation of Plato, Aristotle and Thomas Aquinas, modern science could not have been developed. This exclusion of metaphysics and theology from science does not mean that the use of a certain method of cognition is made the criterion of science; it means that the adequacy of metaphysical-theological speculation is measured by its usefulness to the purpose of science. That this kind of speculations is not only useless to the purpose of science but constitutes a serious obstacle to its progress, is an undeniable fact, shown by the intellectual history of mankind.

It may be argued that the exclusion of metaphysical and theological speculations from science is justified only as far as natural science is concerned; that in the field of social science the recourse to metaphysics and theology – and that means Religion – is admissible and even necessary, because this is the only way to arrive at a solution of the most important problem of that science, the absolute value, implied in the question of what is right and wrong, that is, the question of justice. And indeed it cannot be denied – as pointed out – that on the basis of a social science which abstains from such a recourse no definite answer to the question of justice, excluding any other, can be reached. However, it can be and has been shown that the innumerable attempts which have been made from the earliest times of antiquity until to-day to solve the problem of justice as an absolute value by metaphysical-religious speculation have completely failed. The results of these speculations are of two types only.[11] If the values proclaimed are so substantial that they can be applied to real social relations, they prove to be principles at the basis of a positive social order established under definite economic, political and other cultural conditions of a certain time and a certain space, as, e.g., the absolute values maintained by Christian theology.[12] If, however, they are not of this type, they are empty formulae which by their very nature as transcendental truth exclude any definition that could confer on them a content concrete enough to make them applicable in an unambiguous way to social

[11]Cf. Kelsen, *Was ist Gerechtigkeit?*, Wien, 1953.

[12]Cf. Kelsen, "Die Idee der Gerechtigkeit nach den Lehren der christlichen Theologie." *Studia philosophiae*, Cf. Kelsen, "The Platonic Justice." *Ethics*, 48, (1937/38), pp. 367ff.; as to Aristotle's philosophy of justice: Kelsen, "The Metamorphoses of the Idea of Justice." *Interpretations of Modern Legal Philosophies*. Essays in honor of Roscoe Pound. 1947, pp. 390ff.

reality. Hence they can be, and actually are, used to justify any positive social system whatever. This is exactly the case with the Platonic Agathon, the Aristotelian Nous, the Stoic Logos and the Thomistic *ratio aeterna*, to which Voegelin wants to lead back political science.

After having attributed the destruction worked by "positivism" "in the first place" to the fact that positivistic social science tried to apply the methods of mathematizing natural sciences to social problems, Voegelin admits that "a transfer of methods of mathematical physics in any strict sense of the word to the social sciences has hardly ever been attempted" and declares: "if positivism should be construed in a strict sense as meaning the development of social science through the use of mathematizing methods, one might arrive at the conclusion that positivism has never existed."[13] How could a positivism which – as characterized by Voegelin – never existed, destroy science? Hence Voegelin must divert his attack from an existing positivistic social science to "the intention of making the social sciences 'scientific' through the use of methods which as closely as possible resemble the methods employed in sciences of the external world."[14] If, as Voegelin assumes, this intention has never been realized – otherwise it would be more than a mere "intention" – it can hardly have the destructive effect which justifies the heroic attempt of a restoration of the science of politics. A mere "intention" can have no effect at all. However, the attempt to approach certain problems of social science by using methods similar to those applied in natural science, that is to say, the attempt to find out a causal nexus among social phenomena had led to quite satisfactory results. To mention only two characteristic examples: the relationship which exists between economic facts and political and legal organization, shown by sociologists who follow, with reservations, the Marxian interpretation of society; and the influence of certain religious ideas on forms of economics, demonstrated by Max Weber. No objective critique can deny these achievements.

The use of method as the criterion of science – which, according to Voegelin is one of the fundamental errors of positivism – "abolishes theoretical relevance". Hence positivistic social science is guilty of the "accumulation of irrelevant knowledge." This "is the first of the manifestations of positivism."[15] But this manifestation has nothing to do with positivism. The accumulation of irrelevant knowledge is not necessarily a characteristic of an anti-metaphysical or religiously indifferent science. The accumulation of irrelevant knowledge is avoided by the establishment of a definite criterion of relevance, by determining a certain point of view from where a distinction

---

[13]Voegelin, l.c., p. 4

[14]L.c., p. 7.

[15]L.c., pp. 8,9.

can be made between relevant and irrelevant facts. This is possible without any recourse to metaphysics or religion or the assumption of a "transcendent truth"; and Voegelin does not make any attempt to prove the contrary.

But, as a matter of fact, he does not maintain his accusation that the first manifestation of the destruction of science by positivism is accumulation of irrelevant knowledge. After having ridiculed "the fantastic accumulation of irrelevant knowledge through huge 'research projects' whose most interesting feature is the quantifiable expense that has gone into their production," he admits: "Major research enterprises which contain nothing but irrelevant materials are rare, indeed, if they exist at all. ... Even the staunchest positivist will find it difficult to write a completely worthless book about American constitutional law as long as with any conscientiousness he follows the lines of reasoning and precedents indicated by the decisions of the Supreme Court."[16] This can only mean that in the field of constitutional law – and the same is true as far as all the other fields of political science are concerned – the destructive positivism, against which Voegelin is fighting, simply does not exist.

One of his main objections against this positivism refers even to writings of which he expressly declares that they operate "on relevant materials", that the damage they have done "is not due to an accumulation of worthless materials"; that they, on the contrary, furnish "reliable informations concerning facts."[17] How, then, can the accumulations of irrelevant knowledge be the first manifestation of the destruction of science by positivism? If it is not the accumulation of irrelevant knowledge, what else is wrong with these positivists who, in spite of their destructive effect, operate "on relevant materials" and furnish "reliable informations"? "Their principles of selection and interpretation had no proper theoretical foundation but derived from the *Zeitgeist*, political preferences, or personal idiosyncrasies."[18] How writers who are biased in this way can furnish "reliable informations concerning facts," is difficult to understand. Besides, none of the defects referred to: *Zeitgeist*, political preferences, personal idiosyncrasies, have anything to do with positivism. In his choice of a metaphysical assumption or a theological dogma an anti-positivistic writer my be affected by the Zeitgeist, or political preferences, or personal idiosyncrasies, just as a positivist in his selection or interpretation of the material. As to examples of a positivistic social science built on such improper foundations, Voegelin refers to "the treatises on Plato which discovered in him a precursor of Neo-Kantian logic or according to the political fashions of the time, a constitutionalist, a utopian, a socialist, or

[16]L.c., p. 8, 9.
[17]L.c., pp. 9, 10.
[18]L.c., pp. 9,10.

a Fascist ..."[19] These treatises have been written by authors who belong to the most different schools and some of them were anything else but "positivists." The interpretations of Plato's political philosophy, which Voegelin rejects, are possible from a positivistic as well as from a non-positivistic point of view, and the distinction between a realistic and a utopian or a democratic and autocratic political doctrine may legitimately be applied to a philosophy which Voegelin considers to be of the utmost importance for our time. Besides, the fundamental categories of political thought according to which Plato's political system is interpreted by allegedly destructive positivists are taken from Plato himself, whom Voegelin regards as the founder of a political science[20] to the principles of which we should return. That any of the interpretations of Plato with which Mr. Voegelin does not agree is the result of an undue influence of the *Zeitgeist*, political preferences, or personal idiosyncrasies, is an assertion for which Voegelin does not give the slightest proof.

In the same way, that is without any documentation, he asserts that "histories of political ideas" were "unable to discover much political theory in the Middle Ages" because they "defined politics in terms of Western constitutionalism." Voegelin does not specify these histories and does not show that the historians belonged to the positivistic school of thought; nor does he indicate which positivists "completely ignored the block of political sectarian movements which culminated in the reformation"[21]; which ignorance can certainly not be attributed to an anti-metaphysical attitude of the historian. He then jumps, without any sufficient reason, to Gierke's *Genossenschaftsrecht*, to which he objects that it advocates the "theory of the *Realperson*," which is certainly just the opposite of a positivistic doctrine. After having thus stigmatized the second manifestation by which "science has been destroyed", Voegelin proceeds to the third manifestation. And this is the queerest argument set forth against destructive positivism. It is "the development of methodology, especially in the half-century from 1870 to 1920."[22] Voegelin emphasizes that "the movement was distinctly a phase of positivism" because "the perversion of relevance, through the shift from theory to method, was the very principle by which it lived." But, at the same time he admits: "it was instrumental in overcoming positivism." And how did destructive positivism "overcome" positivism and thus perform a highly constructive function? By insisting on methodological clarification it achieved just that understanding the lack of which Voegelin declared as one

---

[19]L.c., p. 10.
[20]L.c., p. 1.
[21]L.c., p. 10.
[22]L.c., p. 10.

of the "two fundamental assumptions" of "the destruction worked by positivism:" the understanding of the "specific adequacy of different methods for different sciences."[23] If positivism is at the same time destructive and constructive, lacking and gaining the understanding the new science of politics considers as essential, this science is fighting against an imaginary opponent. As representatives of the destructive positivism Voegelin denounces two of the most prominent philosophers of the 20th century: Husserl and Cassirer. But at the same time he recognizes that their works constitute "important steps towards the restoration of theoretical relevance." Nevertheless he maintains, precisely in this connection, his accusation of destruction of science, although he concedes that "the movement as a whole, therefore, is far too complex to admit of generalizations ..." Yet it is just the movement as a whole which Voegelin accuses of having destructed science.

The destruction of science by positivism is – according to Voegelin – due above all to its "attempt at making political science (and the social sciences in general) 'objective' through methodologically rigorous exclusion of all 'value-judgments'."[24] But, on the other hand, he admits that this attempt did "awaken the consciousness of critical standards" and "insofar as the attack on value-judgments was an attack on uncritical opinion under the guise of political science, it had the wholesome effect of theoretical purification."[25] How an intellectual attempt can have the effect of "theoretical purification" and at the same time that of a destruction of science, is difficult to understand. Whatever the effect of this attempt might be, it presupposes the distinction between objective, i.e. verifiable propositions concerning facts and judgments concerning values which, by their very nature, are subjective and hence not scientific. This distinction, Voegelin asserts, is an error due to the fact that the positivistic thinkers "did not master the classic Christian science of man. For neither classic nor Christian ethics and politics contain 'value-judgments' but elaborate, empirically and critically, the problems of order which derive from philosophical anthropology as part of a general ontology. Only when ontology as a science was lost, and when consequently ethics and politics could no longer be understood as sciences of the order in which human nature reaches its maximal actualization, was it possible for this realm of knowledge to become suspect as a field of subjective, uncritical opinion."[26]

The statement that positivistic social science excludes "all" value judgments is a gross misinterpretation of the theory concerned. The term "value

[23] L.c., p. 11.
[24] L.c., p. 11.
[25] L.c., p. 12.
[26] L.c., pp. 11f.

judgment" has – as positivistic writers have pointed out – many meanings. A judgment which most frequently is characterized as a value judgment is the proposition that something is an appropriate means for the realization of a presupposed end. Since the relationship of means to end, as pointed out, coincides with the relation of cause and effect, the proposition in question is objectively verifiable; and if it is – as usually – considered a value judgment, no positivist excludes this value judgment from a scientific theory, because of its "subjectivity." It is a specifically positivistic view that value judgments concerning appropriate means are a special type of propositions concerning facts, and that only judgments to the effect that something ought to be considered as an ultimate end are the value judgments which in the last analysis are based on emotional factors and for this reason subjective and hence relative only. Other judgments which usually are characterized as "value judgments" are propositions by which positive legal and moral orders prescribing a definite human behavior are described in terms of statements about what ought to be done, and propositions by which conformity or non-conformity of actual human behavior with positive law or morality is ascertained. Propositions of this type are the essence of scientific jurisprudence and ethics, which have nothing to do with metaphysics or theology. The methodological postulate that scientific jurisprudence and ethics (including political theory) are to be value-free means only that the description, analysis and explanation of a positive system of law and morality – and only a positive system of norms, that is, a normative order established by acts of human beings and, by and large, applied and obeyed, can be the object of scientific knowledge – should not be influenced by "political preferences or personal idiosyncrasies" of the writer: a principle which – as we have seen – Voegelin himself maintains in his criticism of positivism. Hence it is quite astonishing that the same author, who condemns positivism as destructive because its interpretation of Plato is biased by subjective value judgments on the part of representatives of this school of thought, rejects the distinction between objective propositions concerning facts and subjective value judgments. And even more astonishing is the argument that "neither classic nor Christian ethics and politics" – that is, the metaphysical speculation of Thomas Aquinas – "contain 'value-judgments' ". This is indeed a metaphysical-theological way to argue. A statement is true if in conformity, and false if not in conformity with that what is written in Plato's dialogues or in the Bible. Even if one places the term value judgment between quotation marks, one cannot deny that the statement that a certain human behavior is just or unjust, that is to say, that it ought or ought not to take place, is a value judgment and as such different from the statement that a certain human behavior actually takes place or has taken place; and one cannot deny that the works of Plato as well as those of Christian ethics and politics are full of statements about what is just, that the problem of the value we call justice is their very center. It is precisely the insufficiency of the answer positivism can give to the question of justice by which Voegelin justifies his condemnation of this school of thought.[27] It is true that the value judgments of classic and Christian ethics and politics referring to ultimate ends claim to be objective; but it is just this claim which, examined by a scientific theory of values, proves to be unfounded.

Voegelin seems to assume that Plato's mystic philosophy of the good and the speculations of Christian ethics and politics about divine justice have nothing to do with value judgments because they have the character of "ontology," that is, cognition of the being. But metaphysical ontology is the typical way of presenting subjective values as objective truths. This is confirmed by Voegelin's definition of ontology as a science "of the order in which human nature reaches its maximal actualization."[28] If this phrase has any meaning at all, it can only refer to a normative order; the statement that human nature reaches "maximal actualization" can only mean that if human behavior is in conformity with this order it realizes the highest possible value; and that means the absolute value. That it is the absolute value Voegelin has in mind - although he does not admit it expressly – when he appeals to an ontology, based on metaphysics and theology, results from the fact that he says of the positivistic social science which has "lost" this ontology: "Neither the most scrupulous care in keeping the concrete work 'value-free' nor the most conscientious observation of critical method in establishing facts and causal relations could prevent the sinking of historical and political sciences into a morass of relativism."[29] It is against relativism – that is the view according to which only relative values are accessible to human reason and that, consequently, no scientific decision is possible between economic security as the ultimate end or highest value of Marxism, and individual freedom as the ultimate end or highest value of liberalism – it is just against this philosophy that the "ontology" based on metaphysics and theology is directed. For metaphysical and religious speculations aim by their very nature at the absolute in general and the absolute value in particular.

It is a characteristic tendency of metaphysical-religious speculation to efface the difference between reality and value, between the "is" and the "ought." For reality is according to the fundamental assumption of such speculation the realization of the absolute value: the will of a transcendent authority; which is the assumption that the world is created by God. Only under this presupposition reality and value coincide, is there – in the last

---

[27]L.c., p. 6.
[28]L.c., p. 12.
[29]L.c., p. 13.

analysis – no difference between "is" and "ought." Then, and only then, ontology, the cognition of being, can pretend to be at the same time the cognition of the absolute value. If ontology, as Voegelin asserts, is a science of the order in which human nature reaches its maximal actualization, the question arises which is the order under which such actualization takes place? Marxists assert that it is the social order of communism; their opponents assert that it is the social order of capitalism. Who is right and who is wrong? Is Voegelin really so naive as to believe that a scientific answer to this question can be derived from the Platonic Agathon or the Thomistic *ratio aeterna*? Although everybody agrees with the ideal of a maximal actualization of human nature – since everybody can interpret this vague formula according to his fancy – and although the Platonic as well as the Thomistic formula has long been known, there is still a passionate fight about the right way to its realization. If there were an answer to this question as demonstrable and convincing as a scientific answer has to be, the great conflict of our time would disappear, just as there is no conflict with respect to the question how to build a steam engine or to treat syphilis. If the new science of politics is in the possession of the answer, what is it waiting for? The effect which it would have on the social life of our time would attest its scientific truth. Until the new science of politics discloses its secret, its appeal to the Platonic Agathon or the Thomistic *ratio aeterna* must be considered as idle talk. It will probably object that the question does not allow an answer as clear and unambiguous as natural science can give. Then any of the highly contradictory answers that may be, and actually have been, deduced from the empty formulae of the Platonic Agathon or the Thomistic *ratio aeterna* must be recognized as equally valid. Which means that the metaphysical-religious speculation leads exactly to the same situation which Voegelin so critically characterizes as the "morass of relativism." He thinks that he can strike a deadly blow at positivism by ascertaining that the exclusion of subjective value judgments, and consequently the rejection of the "whole body of classic Christian metaphysics ... could result in nothing less than a confession that a science of human and social order did not exist."[30] If Voegelin understands by a "science of human and social order" the science of social order "in which human nature reaches its maximal actualization," that is to say, the establishment, by science, of a social order guaranteeing the realization of the absolute value, he need not extort a "confession" that such science does not exist. That it does not exist is no secret, and the positivistic science never pretended to be such a science. If it ever existed, it has been destroyed, as Voegelin again and again asserts, otherwise, he could not ask for its "restoration." But as long as this miraculous science of a social order

[30]L.c., p. 12.

in which human nature reaches its maximal actualization is not yet definitely established – and it seems that the new science of politics has the ambition to be or to become such a science – Voegelin must not expect that somebody who has that "consciousness of critical standards" that he considers as desirable can believe in its existence.

The methodological postulate of value-free description and explanation of social phenomena is one of the main elements of Max Weber's positivistic sociology. In order to demonstrate the futility of this postulate, Voegelin tries to show that, if Weber's work is not completely without importance, if it constitutes, in spite of its positivism, at least to a certain extent an "ascent toward essence"[31], it is so because Weber actually – although unintentionally and unconsciously – attributes to science the function of determining values. That means that Weber's work is self-contradictory. The way in which Voegelin achieves this result is significant. He states quite correctly: "A value-free science meant to Weber the exploration of causes and effects, the construction of ideal types that would permit distinguishing regularities of institution as well as deviations from them, and especially the construction of typical causal relations. Such a science would not be in a position to tell anybody whether he should be an economic liberal or a socialist, a democratic constitutionalist or a Marxist revolutionary, but it could tell him what the consequences would be if he tried to translate the values of his preference into political practice."[32] But then he continues: "On the one side, there were the 'values' of political order beyond critical evaluation; on the other side, there was a science of the structure of social reality that might be used as technical knowledge by a politician. ... In the intellectual climate of the methodological debate the 'values' had to be accepted as unquestionable, and the search could not advance to the contemplation of order." For, as Voegelin asserts, "a 'value-free' political science is not a science of order."[33] By "a science of order" he understands a science establishing a normative order constituting absolute values. Weber's sociology certainly does not claim to be the science of an order in which human nature reaches its maximal actualization, that is to say, the science of a normative order constituting an absolute value. But a science which – as the sociology of Weber – has for its object the causal relations in social reality is also a science of order because it is the order of nature, a causal order according to which such science interprets reality. Voegelin's identification of "order" with a normative order of absolute values is unjustified and misleading because it produces the idea – and this is probably the intention of this identification – that outside of this

[31] L.c., p. 15.
[32] L.c., p. 14.
[33] L.c., p. 16.

normative order there is no order, but chaos; which, of course, is not true.

It is incorrect and a misleading interpretation of the postulate of a value-free political science to maintain, as Voegelin does, that from the point of view of such science the values of a political order are "beyond critical evaluation," that these values have "to be accepted as unquestionable." A value-free political science only maintains that the values which a political system tries to realize cannot be confirmed by science as absolute values. That does not mean that a critical evaluation of the political system is impossible; it means only that the recognition of an absolute value is not possible on the basis of a political "science." A value-free political science does not exclude the possibility of scientific judgments concerning the appropriateness of social measures as means for presupposed ends, that is to say, judgments about relative values in the sense explained above; it is far from asserting that political values have to be accepted as unquestionable. Just the contrary is true. It is the "science of order" postulated by Voegelin which insists upon the unquestionable acceptance of values, because this science pretends to prove their absolute validity.

Referring to the teaching of political science at universities, Voegelin states that "the science of Weber" only "supposedly left the political values of the students untouched, since the values were beyond science." In truth, these values are touched, for the political science, in spite of its tendency not to "extend the principles of order" may "have the indirect effect of inviting the students to revise their values when they realized what unsuspected, and perhaps undesired, consequences their political ideas would have in practice." And from this Voegelin concludes: "An appeal to judgment would be possible, and what could be a judgment that resulted in reasoned preference of value over value be but a value judgment? Were reasoned value-judgments possible after all?"[34] The answer has to be in the affirmative. "Reasoned value judgments", that is, value judgments determined by reason and hence scientific value judgments, are possible, even according to Weber's supposedly value-free science.

The situation to which Voegelin refers is that which is correctly described as conflict of values. It is the consequence of the fact that usually not one but two or more values are presupposed as ultimate ends, as for instance, individual freedom and social security, and that the realization of the one proves to be incompatible with the realization of the other. Then a choice between these values is necessary, a decision must be made about which one is preferred to the other.

Science can demonstrate that the means by which a certain end – that is to say a value – is to be realized are inappropriate for the realization of

---

[34] L.c., p. 16.

the other value. This judgment is a reasoned judgment in the sense of a judgment determined by reason, a scientific judgment. For it is a judgment about the relation of cause and effect, and that means a judgment concerning facts. But the judgment according to which one value is to be preferred to another value, is a pure value judgment and it is not at all possible on the basis of scientific reason, as is the judgment concerning the appropriate means. Voegelin concludes from the fact that the judgment according to which the realization of one value is incompatible with the realization of another value is a reasoned judgment, that the judgment according to which one value is to be preferred to another value, too, is a reasoned, that is, scientific judgment. This is a false conclusion. On the basis of this false conclusion he arrives at the following thesis, which has considerable significance for his fight against positivism in general and a value-free political science in particular because it shows the goal at which this new political science is driving: "The teaching of a value-free science of politics in a university would be a senseless enterprise unless it were calculated to influence the values of the students by putting at their disposition an objective knowledge of political reality."[35]

By putting at the disposition of the students an objective knowledge of political reality it is impossible to influence the values of the students. And putting at the disposition of the students an objective knowledge of reality is a highly meaningful enterprise, even if, nay, just because, the choice of the value is left to the students, that is, just because science does not restrict the freedom of this choice. If the student realizes that in his choice of political value, in his decision to support a socialist or a capitalist, a democratic or an autocratic system, he cannot rely on the authority of science that science has not and cannot restrict the freedom of his choice, he will become aware of the fact that he has to make this choice under his own responsibility; which is a highly moral consequence of the value-free science. It is the fear of this responsibility that leads to the tendency to shift the responsibility for the political decision from the subject to an objective authority, to science. And it is a misuse of this weakness of the individual if in totalitarian states the universities have to assume the task of political indoctrination of the students, or, as Voegelin formulates it: "to influence the values of the students." Since this cannot be achieved by an "objective knowledge of political reality," the task of influencing the political values of the students can be fulfilled only by an ideologically distorted knowledge of political reality, that is to say, by a doctrine, which pretends that just that value which the political power, directly or indirectly controlling the university, prefers, is immanent in reality, and hence the only true, the absolute value. That means that the universities become the instruments of politics, and, where they are under the exclusive

[35]L.c., p. 16.

control of the government, a kind of intellectual police. That is exactly what the universities of Nazi-Germany and Fascist Italy have been and the universities of communist Russia still are – in complete conformity with the principle "to influence the values of the students."

Voegelin does not content himself to ascertain the regrettable fact that Max Weber did not "take the decisive step toward a science of order"[36]; he has the ambition to explain why Weber was unable of such an achievement; which amounts to the rather naive question why Weber remained a positivist and did not turn to metaphysics. Among the many astonishing statements, he makes in his fight against positivism, his answer to this question deserves particular notice. Although he must admit that the amount of material Weber mustered in his sociology of religion, "is indeed awe-inspiring," Voegelin considers himself competent to ascertain a gap in Weber's knowledge, "a scientific omission,"[37] as he puts it. If Weber had filled this gap, he would have taken "the decisive step toward a science of order,"[38] that is to say, he had become a metaphysician. This, it is true, Voegelin does not say directly, but it is implied in his following statements. He says immediately after blaming Weber for his omission: "Weber's readiness to introduce verities about order as historical facts stopped short of Greek and medieval metaphysics. In order to degrade the politics of Plato, Aristotle, or St. Thomas to the rank of 'values' among others, a conscientious scholar would first have to show that their claim to be science was unfounded."[39] With the same right one could say that a conscientious scholar who, like Voegelin, summons political science to return to the speculations of metaphysicians, has first to show that the claim of metaphysics to be science is founded, which, of course, he is far from doing. He only asserts that the "attempt [to show that the metaphysical speculations of Plato, Aristotle and Thomas are not science,] is self-defeating. By the time the would-be critic has penetrated the meaning of metaphysical speculation with sufficient thoroughness to make his criticism weighty, he will have become a metaphysician himself." That implies that Weber would have become a metaphysician if he had penetrated the meaning of metaphysics. Voegelin continues: "The attack on metaphysics can be undertaken with a good conscience only from the safe distance of imperfect knowledge." That means: the only reason for not being a metaphysician is imperfect knowledge of metaphysics. This statement, if made without proving that all positivists had only imperfect knowledge of metaphysics – and such proof is of course impossible – has no more weight than the statement

---

[36]L.c., p. 19.
[37]L.c., p. 20.
[38]L.c., p. 19.
[39]L.c., p. 20.

that the only reason for not being a positivist is imperfect knowledge of positivism.

Now, what is the gap which Voegelin discovered in Max Weber's awe-inspiring knowledge of the various religions, the omission which prevented this positivist from becoming a metaphysician? Lo and behold, the knowledge "of pre-Reformatic Christianity."[40] Voegelin has no right to maintain that Weber was ignorant of medieval Christianity the wisdom of which is concentrated in the work of Thomas Aquinas: For his only sole argument could be the fact that Weber did not take into particular consideration pre-Reformation Christianity, which might have many other reasons. Besides, the metaphysics of medieval Christianity is not so different from classic and other Christian metaphysics – Thomas Aquinas' metaphysics is essentially influenced by Aristotle's speculations – that knowledge of classic metaphysics or metaphysics of post-medieval Christianity could not have the same effect of converting a positivist into a metaphysician. It seems that Voegelin anticipated this objection; for he reproaches Weber not only with ignorance of pre-Reformation Christianity but also with the above-mentioned lack of knowledge of Greek metaphysics. Voegelin seriously maintains that Weber has not "seriously occupied himself with Greek philosophy."[41] To maintain that Weber was a positivist because he had no sufficient knowledge of pre-Reformation Christianity and of Plato's and Aristotle's metaphysics is an inadmissible statement, not only because it cannot be proved, but because it implies – as a dogma – the view that classic and Christian metaphysics represent an absolute truth.

Voegelin has not only discovered the omission of pre-Reformation Christianity in Weber's sociology of religion, he knows also the reason of this omission. He says: "The reason of the omission seems to be obvious. One can hardly engage in a serious study of medieval Christianity without discovering among its 'values' the belief in a rational science of human and social order and especially of natural law. Moreover, this science was not simply a belief, but it was actually elaborated as a work of reason. Here Weber would have run into the fact of a science of order ... "[42] How can the reason of the omission be the specific content of the metaphysical speculations concerned if Weber had no knowledge of this content? And if he had the knowledge, he is then guilty of having intentionally omitted dealing with these metaphysical speculations, in order to maintain his positivistic view. If Voegelin does not accept the first-mentioned interpretation of his attack against Weber because it reveals his argument as illogical, he exposes him-

---

[40] L.c., p. 20.
[41] L.c., p. 20.
[42] L.c., p. 20.

self to the suspicion of imputing to a great scholar scientifically improper motives. Perhaps Voegelin did not mean what he actually said, namely, that Weber omitted to take into consideration pre-Reformation Christianity because this material would have shown to him the existence of a science of order and consequently would have forced him to give up his positivistic negation of such a science. Voegelin's idea probably was that if Weber had studied pre-Reformation Christianity, he would have changed his view concerning a science of order. But this assumption would be as inadmissible as the above-mentioned conclusion Voegelin draws from Weber's alleged ignorance of classic metaphysics.

Voegelin asserts that medieval Christianity has elaborated "a rational science of human and social order and especially of natural law", the "science of order" to which he wants to drive back the political science of our time. The core of this science is indeed the natural law. This is nothing particular to the metaphysics of pre-Reformation Christianity. On the contrary. The natural-law doctrine flourished in post-Reformation Christianity, and was very well known to Max Weber. But the question is whether this doctrine, and the entire metaphysical speculation of which it was an essential part, is really a "science", as Voegelin asserts. According to the standard he adopts with respect to the anti-metaphysical attitude of a "conscientious scholar" he is obliged to show that the claim of this metaphysical speculation to be a science is founded; and this all the more as conscientious scholars have submitted the natural-law doctrine again and again to the tribunal of science and the claim has always been dismissed, especially because of the highly contradictory results of this doctrine.[43] But Voegelin is far from complying with this standard.

He quite correctly states that for Max Weber the evolution of mankind toward the rationality of positive science "was a process of disenchantment (*Entzauberung*) and de-divinization (*Entgöttlichung*)."[44] But Voegelin believes that he can hear in Weber's theory "overtones" of a "regret that divine enchantment had seeped out of the world"; that Weber's rationalism was a mere "resignation." I have known Max Weber personally and studied his works very carefully, and on the basis of this knowledge I may say that the "overtones" and the "resignation" exist only in the metaphysical imagination of Voegelin. His imagination was probably stimulated by the laudable wish to mitigate somehow his criticism of a great master and to be able to say finally of Weber: "He saw the promised land but he was not permitted to enter it"[45], which, of course, is the land to which political science will be lead by

[43] Cf. Hans Kelsen, "The Natural-Law Doctrine before the Tribunal of Science.", *The Western Political Quarterly*, II., (1949), pp. 481ff.

[44] Voegelin, l.c., p. 22.

[45] L.c., p. 22.

a new Moses, about whose identity no reader of the *New Science of Politics* can have the slightest doubt.

2.2 A new Theory of Representation

2.2.1 1.

In the Introduction to his book *The New Science of Politics* Prof. Voegelin expresses his "intention of introducing the reader to a development of political science which as yet is practically unknown to the general public ... "[46] It seems to be rather strange that the development of a science which has not remained the secret of an esoteric sect but presented to the public in printed books and articles, could be unknown to those to whom these publications are addressed. And we can hardly believe that Voegelin understands by general public readers who have no scientific background, that he simply intends to popularize the results of a new science of politics, which already exists in form of monographs. His book is just the contrary of a popular presentation of political theory. Even for an expert in this field it is difficult to understand. For one of its peculiarities is that the author describes relatively simple and by no means unknown facts in a complicated language overloaded with superfluous foreign words, especially Greek terms, which are out of place if their use is not necessary to reproduce faithfully the content of classic writings. Since there are English words which perfectly express Voegelins ideas, the embellishment of the new science by words as *agathon*, *Kosmion*, *xynon*, *eidos*, and the like might well be mistaken as an attempt to impress the reader with the great erudition of the author, a device that a scholar of so high a scientific standard as Voegelin does not need.

From the very first chapter, entitled "Representation and Existence", the new science demonstrates its skill in complicating, to the degree of almost complete obscurantism, a problem familiar to every political scientist: that of political representation. In order to explain what this term means, Voegelin thinks it necessary first to deal with a peculiarity of the object of social science, the well-known fact that men living in society interpret their mutual behavior and the relationships constituted by it, and that social science, in describing, and that implies interpreting, the social phenomena, has to take this primary interpretation, the "self-interpretation of society," as Voegelin calls it,[47] into consideration. Natural science, the interpretation of natural phenomena, does not encounter such primary interpretation. A stone does not say to the mineralogist: I am a plant. But the head of a state may say:

[46] L.c., p. 3.

[47] L.c., p. 27.

I am authorized by God to exercise power. Political science in describing the function of this head of state may confirm or reject this primary interpretation. Positivistic political science, e.g., rejects it as an ideological misinterpretation of political reality, whereas Christian metaphysics – to the principles of which the new political science wishes to return – confirms it according to the teaching of the first theologian of Christianity, St. Paul: "There is no authority except from God, and those that exist have been instituted by God."[48] A critical analysis of primary interpretation is an important task of political science.

What Voegelin calls self-interpretation of society is nothing new; but the new science of politics seems to have made a discovery by telling us that "human society is ... a cosmion, illuminated with meaning from within by the human beings who continuously create and bear it as the mode and condition of their self-realization."[49] This description is certainly very poetic, but scientifically not correct. For the self-interpretation is not always illuminating but, on the contrary, obscuring. Voegelin admits that a "critical clarification" of the self-interpretation which social science encounters is a function of this science.[50] And the primary interpretation by man of their social behavior has nothing to do with man's "self-realization," provided that this term has any meaning at all.

Voegelin quite correctly states that when political science begins to interpret social phenomena it starts from the self-interpretation which it finds in its object. He characterizes this method as the Aristotelian procedure.[51] Since, as Voegelin says, political science "inevitably" starts from the self-interpretation of society and proceeds by critical clarification to theoretical concepts[52] and since there was a political science prior to Aristotle's *Ethics* and *Politics*, Aristotle could not have been the first to apply this method. Voegelin refers to Politics 1280a7ff. This is a passage within Aristotle's analysis of the three forms of government: monarchy, aristocracy, polity, and their forms of degeneration: tyranny, oligarchy, democracy. In discussing the limits of oligarchy and democracy "and what is just in each of these states," Aristotle says: "All men have some natural inclination to justice; but they proceed therein only to a certain degree; nor can they universally point out what is absolutely just, as for instance what is equal appears just, and is so; but not to all, only among those who are equals; and what is unequal appears just, and is so; but not to all, only among those who are unequals; which circumstances some people neglect and therefore judge ill; the rea-

[48]Rom. 13, 1.

[49]Voegelin, l.c., p. 27.

[50]L.c., p. 28.

[51]L.c., p. 28, 31.

[52]L.c., p. 28.

son for which is they judge for themselves, and everyone almost is the worst judge in his own cause." This is the distinction between a merely relative and the absolute justice. Aristotle explains the fact that men do not agree about equality as justice: "because they judge ill in their own cause, and also because each party thinks that if they admit what is right in some particulars, they have done justice on the whole ... but what is absolutely just they omit." Then, Aristotle, in order to answer the question as to what is not merely relative but absolute justice, examines the purpose for which civil society was founded. His answer is that civil society is "not founded in the purpose of men's merely living together, but for their living as men ought." This is the usual empty formula, from which Aristotle concludes that "those who contribute most to this end deserve to have greater power in the city than those who are their equals in family and freedom, but their inferiors in civil virtue, or those who excel them in wealth but are below them in worth."[53] This statement amounts to the truism that the rulers shall be virtuous, or that only the virtuous shall be the ruler. On the basis of this principle Aristotle later justifies the hereditary monarchy.[54] The only statement of Aristotle on which Voegelin could base his assumption of a specific "Aristotelian procedure", consisting in a careful distinction between "theoretical concepts and the symbols that are part of reality"[55] is the remark that "some people" neglect that equality is just only in a relative, not in an absolute sense, that they "judge ill" because "they judge for themselves and everyone almost is the worst judge in his own cause." It is very doubtful whether Aristotle's criticism of the doctrine that equality is justice – which is the basis of democracy – was meant as a "critical clarification of socially pre-existing symbols" [56]; and as an attack on the political theory prevailing in democratic Athens. But even if it is admitted that it was a clarification of a self-interpretation of society, it cannot be denied that Aristotle applied this method only in this connection. In defining his concepts of the three forms of government and their degenerations, he says nothing that could be interpreted as the "Aristotelian method" in the sense of Voegelin. Aristotle states: "We usually call a state which is governed by one person for the common good, a kingdom, one that is governed by more than one, but by a few only, an aristocracy; either because the government is in the hands of the most worthy citizens, or because it is the best form for the city and its inhabitants. When the citizens at large govern for the public good, it is called a polity; which is also a common name for all other governments, and these distinctions are conso-

[53] 1281a.

[54] 1284b, 1288a. Cf. Hans Kelsen, "The Philosophy of Aristotle and the Hellenic-Macedonian Policy." Ethics, 48 (1937), pp. 1ff.

[55] Voegelin, l.c., p. 31.

[56] L.c., p. 28.

nant to reason; for it will not be difficult to find a person, or a very few, of distinguished abilities, but almost impossible to meet with the majority of a people eminent for every virtue." Further, he says: "the corruptions attending each of these governments are these; a kingdom may degenerate into a tyranny, an aristocracy into an oligarchy, and a state into a democracy. Now a tyranny is a monarchy where the good of one man only is the object of government, an oligarchy considers only the rich, and a democracy only the poor; but neither of them have a common good in view."[57] Here Aristotle does evidently not start from the judgment people render in their own cause – if that means self-interpretation of society. On the contrary. He starts from a concept of democracy which is evidently not the symbol used in political reality, the self-interpretation of a democratic society. He begins his definition with the formula "We usually call ... ", pretending that the following definitions are those used in political debates of daily life. But the governments which presented themselves as democracies did not at all use this term to designate a government that has no common good in view, a degenerated corrupted government. Aristotle imputes to the term democracy a meaning which it certainly had not in political reality, and he uses this device not for the scientific purpose of an objective analysis, but for the political purpose the tendency of which was directed against democracy; for aristocracy and especially for monarchy. If there is a specifically "Aristotelian procedure" at all, it is the one which manifests itself in his definition of democracy.

Voegelin formulates as a methodological postulate of the new science of politics: "theoretical concepts and the symbols that are part of reality must be carefully distinguished."[58] Confusion which consists in taking "symbols used in political reality" for "theoretical concepts"[59] must be avoided. It is, however, hardly possible to separate completely a scientific interpretation of social phenomena from the primary or self-interpretation which is implied in the object of political science. For the primary interpretation is more or less influenced by the existing political science, and political science – as a social phenomenon, especially when it intends to serve as a political instrument – to a certain degree becomes the object of political science. Voegelins presentation is itself an example of the confusion of the two kinds of interpretation, and thus shows how easily the distinction he postulates may be omitted. He refers to the "Marxian idea of the realm of freedom, to be established by a communist revolution"[60] He has probably in mind the doctrine set forth by Marx, and especially by Engels in his *Anti-Duehring*[61] that

---

[57] 1279a, b.

[58] L.c., p. 31.

[59] L.c., p. 29.

[60] L.c., p. 29, ibid.

[61] Friedrich Engels, *Herrn Eugen Duehrings Umwälzung der Wissenschaft*, 10th ed., 1919, p.

the progress to communism is "der Sprung der Menschheit aus dem Reich der Notwendigkeit in das Reich der Freiheit" (the leap of mankind from the realm of necessity into the realm of freedom). This is a concept of the theory developed by Marx and Engels, a theoretical concept. This theory and its description of the communist society as a realm of freedom may be rejected as erroneous theory by another social theory; but even a wrong theory is a theory and its concepts are theoretical concepts, because intended to serve as a description and explanation of reality. Voegelin deals with the Marxian concept of the realm of freedom as with a symbol used in political reality because it is part of the Marxian movement. But it is so only because the Marxian theory is used in the reality of the Marxian movement and it is as such the object of a critical theory; just as the theory of Thomas Aquinas is used by the Church in the political reality of a social movement which – like the socialist movement – may be the object of a critical theory. This is the so-called critique of ideology. The fact that a theoretical concept is used in political reality and thus is a symbol of self-interpretation of society does not and cannot deprive it of its character as theoretical concept. Voegelin takes a concept of the Marxian theory as a symbol of self-interpretation of society; and he can do so because the idea of a "realm of freedom" is both. On the basis of his critique of the Marxian theory as an ideology of the socialist movement, Voegelin states that "the symbol 'realm of freedom' is useless in critical science"[62] But that does not mean that it is not a theoretical concept; unless Voegelin assumes that only a correct doctrine is a "theory", and that means that only a doctrine which expresses the absolute truth is a "theory" in the solely admissible use of the term. Under this assumption no theory at all has come into existence until now. The history of science is the history of a permanent change and transformation of theories, of a process in which one theory is replaced as erroneous by another theory, which inevitably will have the same fate. Nevertheless, Voegelin seems to proceed from the assumption that only a correct theory is a theory. He exhorts political science so passionately to return to the principles of the classic and Christian metaphysics because he believes that there we may find the absolute truth. He should not ignore that the doctrine of the ideas, which is the core of Plato's metaphysics and which culminates in the idea of the absolute good (the *agathon*), was refuted in the metaphysics of Aristotle as a superfluous reduplication of the object of cognition, and, hence, may be considered – from this point of view – just as the Marxian realm of freedom from the point of view of Voegelin's metaphysics – as "useless in critical science."

The danger which results from the parallelism of the interpretation of

306.

[62]Voegelin, l.c., p. 29.

social reality used in this reality, and the interpretation of social reality by political science is not that the self-interpretation of society is taken to be a "theory". For it may indeed be a theory although a theory to be rejected by political science. The decisive difference between the two interpretations is not that the one is, whereas the other is not, a theory, but the fact that the interpretation of social reality by political science ought to be, and can be, objective, whereas the self-interpretation of society, although it, too, pretends to be objective, is necessarily more or less subjective, that is to say, determined by the social interests of the interpreting subject. This difference, to be sure, is only a relative one. There is no other science in which the fulfillment of the requirement of objectivity is so difficult as in political science. The greater therefore is the danger that political science will uncritically take over the political theory used in political reality by those who exercise political power, that is to say by governments or by groups opposed to the government, as a political instrument, and thus becomes itself a political instrument. This is the real danger of political science: that it gives up the attempt to be objective. And the danger is unavoidable if political science refuses to be "value-free." For, if a political science identifies itself with a definite political value, and that means with a definite political system, it inevitably is degraded to a handmaid of politics. Then there can be not one political science as there is only one science of biology, but there must be always at least two sciences of politics, advocating opposite political values, the results of the one being as "true" as those of the other.

Since the new science of politics expressly refuses to be a value-free interpretation of political reality, it is quite understandable that it is not at all this danger which, according to Voegelin, is of importance. Instead, he emphasizes the distinction between theoretical concepts and symbols used in political reality. But just as he ignores this distinction by taking a theoretical concept – the Marxian realm of freedom – as a symbol used in political reality, he also takes symbols used in political reality as theoretical concepts.

In his analysis of the development of the concept of representation he refers to the Magna Carta, the writs of summons of the 13th and 14th century, the address of Henry VIII to parliament in Ferrer's case, two treatises of Sir John Fortescue, the *History of the Lombards* of Paulus Diaconus, and professor Haurious's *Precis de Droit constitutionnel.*[63] The concepts used in the Magna Charta, the writs of summons, the address of Henry VIII are symbols of self-interpretation of society; the concepts presented in the works of Fortescue, Paulus Diaconus, and Hauriou are symbols of political science. There is not the slightest difference in the treatment of these sources by Voegelin's new political science. He takes the concept "the king in Par-

[63]L.c., pp. 38ff.

liament"[64] used in the address of Henry VIII just as Fortescue's doctrine that "all that the king does ought to be referred to his kingdom"[65] as a contribution to the theory of representation; and he considers the definition of Parliament as "the *commune consilium regni nostri*" in the Magna Carta just as important to political science as Prof. Haurious's definition of the concept of representation.[66]

Voegelin first discusses the "elemental aspects" of representation.[67] The aspect is elemental but it is "theoretically" elemental. Voegelin states expressly that he speaks "of the theoretically elemental aspect"[68] of his topic, and refers to "the theoretization of representative institutions" on the elemental level.[69] We must remember that Voegelin just before has insisted on the sharp distinction between theoretical concepts and symbols used in political reality. But now he characterizes the concept of representation used as "a symbol in political reality"[70] as the theoretically elemental aspect of representation, and by use "in political reality" he understands here the use of the term representation "in political debate, in the press, and in the publicist literature."[71] Since publicist literature implies books on political science, the distinction between symbols used in political reality, i.e. symbols of self-interpretation of society and theoretical concepts is abandoned. And the way in which Voegelin describes the meaning "representation" has in political reality is precisely the way in which traditional political science defines the concept of representation or, more exactly, of democratic representative institutions such as election of the legislative and the main executive organs of the state on the basis of a universal and free suffrage.[72] After declaring this aspect of the problem as the theoretically elemental aspect, he asks: "What can the theorist do with an answer of this type in science? Does it have any cognitive value?" Voegelin's answer is not directly in the negative. But he attributes to the elemental concept of representation only little cognitive value. This is the reason why he thinks it necessary to replace it by a concept of greater cognitive value, the "existential" type of representation.

But why is the definition of representation as a system of government according to which the organs of the state are elected on the basis of universal and free suffrage "elemental" and why has it only little cognitive value? Be-

---

[64]L.c., p. 39
[65]L.c., p. 45
[66]L.c., pp. 48f.
[67]L.c., pp. 31ff.
[68]L.c., p. 31.
[69]L.c., p. 33.
[70]L.c., p. 32.
[71]L.c., pp. 31,32.
[72]L.c., p. 32.

cause it refers only to the "external existence of society"[73], "to simple data of the external world"[74], because it "casts light only on an area of institutions within an existential framework", whereas "the framework itself remains in the shadow."[75] It is evidently the "existential framework" that Voegelin considers as essential, not the "external existence of society." But what does he understand by the existential framework and where does representation take place unless within the external existence of society? If – as Voegelin seems to assume – the "external existence of society" is its existence in "the external world", where else can society, as an aggregate of inter-human relations, exist but in the external world? External existence of society can be only the existence from the point of view of the social scientist. Society as object of social science does not exist – as his ideas or feelings do – within the scientist, but in the external world, that is to say, in a world which from the viewpoint of an objective science is supposed to exist outside the scientist. Hence only the external existence of society comes into the consideration of a social science. If there is, in contradistinction to the external existence, also an internal existence of society, it could be only society in its primary interpretation by men living in society or – as Voegelin puts it – society in its self-interpretation, society as "a cosmion illuminated from within", a cosmion which "has its inner realm of meaning"[76] But, as Voegelin admits, "this realm exists tangibly in the external world in human beings who have bodies and through their bodies participate in the organic and inorganic externality of the world."[77] There is no sufficient reason to disparage a concept of representation as elemental because it refers to "the external existence of society", for a scientific of concept of representation can refer only to the external existence of society; and, as a matter of fact, the final definition of representation presented by Voegelin – the "existential", not the "elemental" aspect of the problem, as he calls it – refers, as we shall see, to exactly the same external existence of society as the elemental definition.

What, then, is the real reason for presenting the definition of a representative form of government as a government elected by the people on the basis of universal suffrage as merely elemental, to be replaced by a more appropriate one, the "existential" definition?

The allegedly elemental definition of representation is the definition of a certain type of representation: representation of a community organized by a democratic constitution. It is of importance to note that the type of representation which the new science of politics depreciates as elemental is that

[73] L.c., p. 31.
[74] L.c., p. 33.
[75] L.c., pp. 34, 33.
[76] L.c., p. 31.
[77] Ibid.

sort of representation which is the essence of democracy. This is not the only possible type of representation. The statement that an individual "represents" a community means that the individual is acting as an organ of the community, and he is acting as an organ of the community when he fulfills certain functions determined by the social order constituting the community. If the order, as in the case of the state, is a legal order, the functions determined by this order are the creation and application of the order. It stands to reason that the legal order must be a valid order; and it is valid if it is, by and large, effective. Only if an individual acts as an organ of the state can his action be imputed to the state, that is, to the community constituted by the legal order; and that means that his action can be interpreted as an action of the state, and the acting individual as a representative of the state. The legal order determines not only the function but also the individual who has to fulfill the function, the organ. There are different methods of determining the organ. If the organ is to be an assembly of the individuals subjected to the legal order, or individuals elected by these individuals, a democracy, and that means a democratic type of representation, is established. But the community, especially the state, is represented not only if it is organized as a democracy. An autocratic state, too, is represented by organs, although they are not determined in a democratic way. Since any organized community has organs, there is representation whenever there exists an organized community, especially a state. It seems that the new science accepts this view. It calls the "process in which human beings form themselves into a society for action" "the articulation of society"[78] Existential representation is "the result of political articulation." To represent a society means to "act for the society" and that means that the acts of the representative are imputed to the society as a whole and not to the acting individual. "When his acts are effectively imputed in this manner, a person is the representative of a society"[79]

However, in a modern so-called representative democracy the organs are considered by traditional political theory to represent the state by representing the people of the state. The statement that the parliament or the president in a democratic state represent the people means nothing else but that the individuals subjected to the legal order constituting the state have a decisive influence on the creation of the legislative and executive organs in question, insofar as the constitution authorizes them to elect these organs. It is true that representation of the state and representation of the people of the community are two different concepts, which traditional political theory does not always distinguish clearly enough. But there can be no doubt about the meaning of the statements concerned when traditional political theory refers to rep-

[78]L.c., p. 37.

[79]Ibid.

resentative institutions. As is so frequently the case, one and the same term is used in a wider as well as in a narrower sense. Just as "constitutional" monarchy indicates a monarchy which has a specific , namely, a more or less democratic constitution, although an absolute monarchy, too, has a constitution and thus is, in this sense, also a constitutional monarchy. The term "representative institutions" signifies a democratic type of representation, although there exists also a non-democratic type of representation. Just as there is no state without a constitution, although the term constitution is used also in a narrower sense, only for a special type of constitution, there is no state without representation, although the term representation is used also in a narrower sense, for a specific type of representation. To use a term in a wider and in a narrower sense is not the best terminological practice, but there is nothing "elemental" in it.

Much more important than the double meaning of representation out of which hardly any misunderstanding can arise, is the fact that the term representation can claim to mean not only representation of the state but at the same time representation of the people of the state: only and exclusively if it refers to representation by organs elected in a democratic way. For if the statement that a state organ represents the people is not to imply a gross fiction, it can mean nothing else but that the individuals subjected to the legal order constituting the state are entitled to exercise decisive influence on the creation of the organs. It is already a fictitious interpretation to say that the will of the organ is identical with the will of the people, especially if the organ is not bound in the discharge of his function by instructions given to him by his electorate, not to speak of the highly problematical character of the so-called will of the people where the people, that is, the electorate is divided in two or more antagonistic parties. It is certainly a still more inadmissible fiction to say of an autocratically established organ, that is to say, an organ on the creation of which the subjects of the state have no influence at all, that it is a representative, not only of the state, but also of the people of the state. The new science of politics seems not to be interested in avoiding this fiction.

In order to proceed from the elemental to the existential type of representation Voegelin maintains that "the elemental type of representative institutions" – that is representation by organs elected on the basis of universal and free suffrage – "does not exhaust the problem of representation." This is certainly true. As pointed out, there exists not only a democratic but also a non-democratic type of representation. But this does not justify considering the former as elemental. The new science itself characterizes the democratic type of representation as representation in a "constitutional" sense[80],

[80]For instance, l.c., p. 49.

though the non-democratic type is also constitutional, since any type of representation must be established by the constitution. Thus the new science of politics uses the term constitution in the same way as the old political science uses the term representation: in a narrower sense, although the term has also a wider sense. It is for another reason that the new science of politics considers the democratic type of representation as elemental. It is elemental because it is – according to the new science – meaningless. The way in which the democratic process is described by Voegelin is quite significant. "In the theoretization of representative institutions on this [elemental] level", says Voegelin, "the concepts which enter into the construction of the descriptive type refer to simple data of the external world. They refer to geographical districts, to human beings who are resident in them, to men and women, to their age, to their voting which consists in placing check marks on pieces of paper by the side of names printed on them, to operations of counting and calculation that will result in the designation of other human beings as representatives, to the behavior of representatives that will result in formal acts recognizable as such through external data, etc."[81] The tendency of the description is evident. The democratic process is presented as something that has no bearing on the essence of the phenomenon in question. It has only a formal character; it is of secondary importance. "The procedure of representation is meaningful only when certain requirements concerning its substance are fulfilled."; "the establishment of the procedure does not automatically provide the desired substance."[82] By "the establishment of the procedure" only the election procedure can be meant. And if it is not the democratic procedure which by itself provides the desired "substance," then, perhaps, a non-democratic procedure may provide it. Thus everything depends on the meaning of the "substance." But what is the meaning of the substance? Since the elemental concept of representation is to be replaced by the existential concept, probably something like "existence." When Voegelin rejects the elemental concept of representation as having only little "cognitive value,"[83] he says that the existence of the democratic countries, the representative institutions of which are described in this elementary way by referring to the fact that their organs are elected by the people, "must be taken for granted without too many questions about what makes them exist or what existence means."[84] This statement can only express the idea that the definition of democratic representation as representation by elected organs is worthless because election of the organs by the

[81] L.c., p. 33.
[82] L.c., p. 35.
[83] L.c., p. 32.
[84] Ibid.

people does not – in itself – guarantee the existence, or a satisfactory existence, of the state. Voegelin's critique of the so-called elemental concept of representation confuses two different questions: the question as to what is democratic representation, and the question as to whether democratic representation assures the existence or satisfactory existence of the state. It is the confusion of the essence of a political phenomenon with its value; and this confusion is a serious methodological error. With respect to the "substance" of representation, Voegelin says that "certain mediatory institutions, the parties, have something to do with securing or corrupting this substance" and that "the substance in question is vaguely associated with the will of the people, but what is meant by the symbol 'people' does not become clear. This symbol must be stored away for later examination."[85] However – as we shall see – the symbol "people" does not become clearer by Voegelin's later examination. On the contrary. It becomes "mysterious", a "mystical substance."[86] Yet this, perhaps, seems to be clear: the existential representation at which the new science of politics is driving, claims to be a representation of the people, although the symbol "people" may mean something different from what it means in the elemental concept of representation, i.e., the electorate. As far as the "mediatory institutions, the parties ... securing or corrupting this substance" are concerned, we learn that "the disagreement on the number of parties that will, or will not, guarantee the flow of the substance suggests an insufficiently analyzed ulterior issue that will not come into grasp by counting parties."[87] Voegelin refers to the fact that there exists a variety of opinion concerning the effect of political parties on the working of a representative system that he summarizes as follows: "a representative system is truly representative when there are no parties, when there is one party, when there are two or more parties, when the two parties can be considered factions of one party ... a representative system will not work if there are two or more parties who disagree on points of principle."[88] By a "representative system" he understands in this connection a system of democratic representation. Here, again, he confuses the question as to the essence of democratic representation with the question under what conditions a democratic system works satisfactorily. That political parties are possible in a democracy, and that a constitution which does not allow the free formation of political parties, which allows either no party at all or only one party, is not democratic, cannot be, and has never been denied by those who are of the opinion that parties are, or are not, advantageous for the working of a

[85]L.c., p. 35.
[86]L.c., p. 43, 44.
[87]L.c., p. 35.
[88]Ibid.

democratic system. The view that only one party is to be allowed in order to guarantee the workability of the government is a common element of the anti-democratic ideologies of fascism, national-socialism and communism; fascist Italy, national-socialist Germany have been, and communist Russia still is, typical "one-party states." This term can have no other meaning. For if the constitution, as in a democracy, guarantees free formation of political parties, the coming into existence of more than one party is inevitable. A democracy cannot be a one-party state. Until now, we were of the opinion that there is a vital difference between a political system which allows only one party, the one supporting the government, and a political system under which the formation of parties is free; and that in a one-party state where there are no free elections because the citizens can vote only for the candidate of one party, the government cannot be considered as representing the people. But the new science of politics informs us that "a type concept like the 'one-party state' must be considered as theoretically of dubious value; it may have some practical use for brief reference in current political debate, but it is obviously not sufficiently clarified to be of relevance in science. It belongs to the elemental class like the elemental type concept of representative institutions."[89] But a one-party state, as we shall see, may offer an ideal case of "existential" representation.

The most characteristic type of a one-party state is the Soviet Union. Voegelin says of this state: "While there may be radical disagreement on the question whether the Soviet government represents the people, there can be no doubt whatsoever that the Soviet government represents the Soviet society as a political society in form for action in history"[90] He does not state in an unambiguous way that the Soviet government does not represent the Soviet people; he does not say that it represents the Soviet state, and not the Soviet people. The only thing he decidedly asserts is that the Soviet government represents the Soviet "society." But by "Soviet society" the soviet people may be understood. For, in order to show that the Soviet government represents the Soviet society, he refers to the fact that the "legislative and administrative acts of the Soviet government are domestically effective in the sense that the governmental commands find obedience with the people ... " and that "the Soviet government can effectively operate an enormous military machine fed by the human and material resources of the Soviet society." The soviet government represents the Soviet society because it effectively controls the Soviet people. In this connection Voegelin says: "under the title of political societies in form for action the clearly distinguishable power

[89]L.c., p. 36.
[90]Ibid.

units in history come into view."[91] These "power units" are usually called states. But why does the new science avoid this term? Why does it not clearly distinguish representation of the state from representation of the people? "Political societies," says Voegelin "in order to be in form for action, must have an internal structure that will enable some of its members – the ruler ... to find habitual obedience for their acts of command; and these acts must serve the existential necessities of a society, such as the defense of the realm and administration of justice."[92]

It is a generally recognized principle that a body of individuals, in order to be considered as the government of a state, must be independent of other state governments and able to obtain for the legal order under which it is acting as government the permanent obedience of the subjects. This principle applies to any government, whether democratic or autocratic. The principle is only a particular application of the more general principle that the legal order constituting the state is valid only if it is by and large effective, that is to say, obeyed by the individuals whose behavior it regulates. It seems that the new science of politics presents this principle, taken for granted by the old political and legal science, under the term of "existential" representation. For it declares "defense" and "administration of justice" as "the existential necessities of a society" and states: the "process in which human beings form themselves into a society for action shall be called the articulation of a society. As the result of political articulation we find human beings, the rulers, who can act for the society, men whose acts are not imputed to their own persons but to the society as a whole – with the consequence that, for instance, the pronunciation of a general rule regulating an area of human life will not be understood as an exercise in moral philosophy but will be experienced by the members of the society as the declaration of a rule with obligatory force for themselves. When his acts are effectively imputed in this manner, a person is the representative of a society."[93] In this context "representation" presupposes effective imputation, which can only mean that the imputation to the state of the acts of the ruler takes place only if the rule is effective.

It is evident that the principle according to which the legal order constituting the state is valid only if it is to a certain extent effective, has no direct relation to the question of representation, that is to say, to the determination by the legal order of the organs of the community constituted by this order, the individuals competent to represent the state. Only a valid legal order can determine the representatives, and only a relatively effective legal order is

---

[91] Ibid.

[92] L.c., p. 36f.

[93] L.c., p. 37.

valid. The principle of effectiveness refers to the legal order constituting the state, not the organs of the state. It is not the organs who are effective, it is the norms created and applied by them in conformity with a valid legal order which are to be effective. That the government is effective means that the norms which are issued by this organ and which form part of the legal order constituting the state are effective. The acts performed by an organ of the state and especially by the government are acts of the state, that is to say, imputable to the state, and, hence the individual performing the acts represents the state, not because the organ is effective, but because the individual and his act is determined by a valid, and that means by a relatively effective legal order. Since only a valid, that is, relatively effective legal order constitutes the community called state, only on the basis of such a legal order organs of a state and, therefore, representation is possible, whether it is democratic or non-democratic representation, representation of the state which is or is not at the same time representation of the people. Effectiveness - as a quality of the constituent order – is a condition of any type of representation, because a condition of the existence of the state. Whether a body of individuals, as the government of a state, represents the state, and at the same time the people of the state, does not depend on the effectiveness of the commands, that is, the norms, which it issues; for any body of individuals is the government of a state only if it acts in conformity with an effective legal order constituting the state, whether democratic or autocratic, and if the norms issued by this body, forming an essential part of the legal order, are by and large obeyed. Whether a government, which always represents the state, represents also the people of the state, that is to say, whether it is a democratic government, depends only and exclusively on the answer to the question whether or not it is established in a democratic way, that is to say, elected on the basis of universal and free suffrage. Hence it is impossible to differentiate the democratic type of representation from any other type of representation by the criterion of effectiveness. But this is just what the new science of politics endeavors. It is just the differentiation at which the new science aims when it deprecates the democratic type of representation as elemental because it does not – as does the existential type – imply the element of effectiveness. Only by obliterating the difference between representation of the state and representation of the people can the new science maintain that there exists a difference of cognitive value between democratic representation, as a merely "elemental" representation, and representation of the state, as an "existential" representation. By obliterating this difference, by avoiding the term "representation of the state", by using the ambiguous formula "representation of society", the new science creates the impression that only that concept of representation which includes the element of effectiveness is the correct one, and that this type of representation always implies, in some way, representation of the people. "Obviously", says the author of the new science, "the representative ruler of an articulated society cannot represent it as a whole without standing in some sort of relationship to the other members of society.." By "the other members of society" only the people can be understood. "... under pressure of the democratic symbolism, the resistance to distinguishing between the two relations terminologically has become so strong that it has also affected political theory ... . The government represents the people, and the symbol 'people' has absorbed the two meanings which, in medieval language, for instance, could be distinguished without emotional resistance as the 'realm' and the 'subjects'."[94] The "two relations" which under the pressure of democratic symbolism are not distinguished, are the relationship of the ruler to society as a whole and the relationship of the ruler to "the other members of society." The statement that the government in a democracy represents the people as subjected to the government means that the government, by representing the people as the society not including the members of the government – "the other members of society" – represents the society as a whole, because the members of the government belong to the people as subjected to the government. They are at the same time governing and subjected to the government. As members of the government they are not – as is the ruler in an autocracy – exempt from the government, they are at the same time governing and subjected to the government. It is just for this reason that only in a democracy the government represents the society as a whole, because it represents the society including the members of the government. But it is very likely that the new science of politics understands by "society as a whole" the state. For this term is supposed to mean about the same as, in medieval language, the term "realm", in contradistinction to the "subjects." This terminology corresponds to the modern distinction between "state" and "people." The statement that a democratic government represents the people does indeed mean that the government representing the people represents the state. Again we ask: Why does the new science refrain from using the modern term "state," which is much less ambiguous than the medieval "realm" literally meaning "kingdom"? Why does it speak of "society as a whole" when it really means state? Evidently because representation of society as a whole implies necessarily representation of "the members of society", because the existential representative of the state has to be considered as representing also the people. "The representative ruler of an articulated society" can only be a ruler who effectively represents society; and if he effectively represents society, he represents it "as a whole", especially if "society as a whole" means "state." It can only be the society as a whole which a ruler in the existential sense – an "existential" ruler –

[94] L.c., p. 38.

represents; and by the representative ruler of an articulate society, referred to in the above-quoted statement, obviously an existential ruler is meant. But every government – whether democratic or autocratic – is a ruler in the existential sense, an existential ruler. And, now, the new science of politics declares that the representative ruler of an articulated society cannot represent it as a whole – and that probably means: cannot represent the state – without standing in some sort of relationship to the other members of the society, that is to say, to the people. That he stands in a relationship to the people can only mean that he represents the people; For representation of the people is one of the two relations terminologically not distinguished "under pressure of the democratic symbolism." The ruler must stand "in some sort" of relationship to the other members of the society, that is to the people, but not necessarily in that sort which is constituted by elections on the basis of universal and free suffrage. For this sort of relationship is only elemental, not existential. The Soviet government, as the new science asserts, "represents the Soviet society as a political society" in the most effective way because the "legislative and administrative acts of the Soviet government are domestically effective in the sense that the governmental commands find obedience with the people" and it "can effectively operate an enormous military machine fed by the human and material resources of the Soviet society."[95] That can only signify that the Soviet government represents the Soviet society "as a whole," especially if "society as a whole" means state. Hence the Soviet government is the ideal type of an existential ruler, a "representative" ruler of an articulated society, represented "as a whole" by the ruler. If a representative ruler of an articulated society "cannot represent it as a whole without standing in some sort of relationship to the other members of the society,"[96] that is to say, without representing in some way the people, then the Soviet government, which is certainly not a democratic government, represents the Soviet people. This, of course, is not expressly maintained by the new science of politics. But it is clearly implied in its doctrine of representation, with its tendency to belittle the importance of the democratic type of representation as merely elemental and to put in the foreground the existential type, in which the principle of effectiveness is emphasized.

Voegelin refers to the fact that in the Magna Carta the Parliament is designated as "the common council of our realm," which probably means – expressed in modern terminology – as an organ of the state, and, as he emphasizes, "not perhaps as a representation of the people;"[97] which is not astonishing since the Magna Carta was not the constitution of a democracy.

---

[95] L.c., p. 36.
[96] L.c., p. 38.
[97] Ibid.

Then Voegelin refers to the writs of summons of the 13th and 14th centuries and ascertains that they draw "the new participants of representation into the royal representation itself. Not only is the realm the king's but the prelates, the magnates, and the cities are also his. ... The symbol 'people' does not appear as signifying a rank in articulation and representation; it is only used, on occasion, as a synonym for realm in a phrase like the 'common welfare of this realm'."[98] Then he quotes the following sentence from the address of Henry VIII to Parliament in Ferrers' case: "We be informed by our Judges that we at no time stand so highly in our estate royal as in the time of Parliament, wherein we as head and you as members are conjoined and knit together into one body politic, so as whatsoever offense or injury (during that time) is offered to the meanest member of the House is to be judged as done against our person and the whole Court of Parliament."[99] That means – expressed in modern language – that the king and each member of the Parliament is to be considered as representing the Parliament. There is no question of a representation of the people.

The "representation of the people" appears only when Voegelin quotes Lincoln's formula of a "government of the people, by the people, for the people."[100] Voegelin says that with this formula "the limit is reached where the membership of the society has become politically articulate down to the last individual, and, correspondingly, the society becomes representative of itself." The "limit" of articulation – meaning organization – is reached when the legislative and the main executive organs are to be elected on the basis of free and universal suffrage, that is to say, when representation in the elemental sense is established. This is, without the slightest doubt, the tenor of Lincoln's formula. And if this formula is – as Voegelin here admits – a "masterful, dialectical concentration, an unsurpassable fusion of democratic symbolism with theoretical content," why did Voegelin, some pages before say, that the "theorist" cannot do very much with the elemental concept of representation, that it has no or not enough "cognitive value"? And, indeed, he is not satisfied with this masterful and unsurpassed formula. For he thinks further clarification is necessary. This clarification he finds in the works of Sir John Fortescue who, in the 15th century published *The Governance of England* and his famous *De laudibus legum Anglie*. What are the important contributions made by this writer to the theory of representation, to the existential, not the elemental, representation? First, his creation of the concepts of "eruption" and "proruption"[101] Fortescue simply says: "*ex populo*

[98] L.c., p. 39.

[99] L.c., p. 40.

[100] Ibid.

[101] L.c., pp. 42f.

erumpit regnum"[102], the kingdom emerged from the people. But Voegelin says: "Fortescue coined the term 'eruption' as a technical term for designating the initial articulation of a society."[103], which is a rather imaginative interpretation of Fortescue's simple statement. The term "proruption" is used by Fortescue in the following sentence: "... *regnum Anglie ... in dominium politicum et regale prorupit* ... " (the kingdom of England was transformed into a dominium regal and political). The terms "eruption" and "proruption" have no specifically technical significance. They do not allow us "to distinguish" – as Voegelin asserts – "the component in representation that is almost forgotten wherever the legal symbolism of the following centuries came to predominate in the interpretation of political reality,"[104] namely, the principle of effectiveness. Voegelin interprets Fortescue's statement in which the term "proruption" is used to designate the transformation of a dominion royal into a dominion royal and political to mean: "a realm will be achieved only when a head is erected, *rex erectus est*, that will rule the body." This, however, is not what Fortescue means by this statement. He says: "A king of England cannot, at his pleasure, make any alterations in the laws of the land, for the nature of his government is not only regal, but political. Had it been merely regal, he would have a power to make what innovations and alterations he pleased, in the laws of the kingdom, impose tollages and other hardships upon the people, whether they would or no, without their consent ... but it is much otherwise with a king, whose government is political, because he can neither make any alteration, or change in the laws of the realm without the consent of the subject, nor burthen them, against their wills, with strange impositions ... "[105] That the government of England is transformed from a *dominium regale* into a *dominium politicum et regale* means that the government of England is transformed from an absolute into a limited monarchy. This is the main point in the work that Fortescue wrote for the instruction of a prince. The terminological distinction of eruption and proruption is of no importance at all. It is certainly not – as Voegelin maintains – a "theoretical achievement."[106]

Another achievement of Fortescue is, according to Voegelin, that "he transferred the Christian symbol of the *corpus mysticum* to the realm."[107] Voegelin admits that Fortescue calls the realm, that is, the state a *corpus mysticum* "only analogically." But he adds: "The *tertium comparationis*

[102]Fortescue, *De laudibus legum Anglie*, chap. XIII.

[103]Voegelin, l.c., p. 42.

[104]L.c., p. 43.

[105]Fortescue, *Commendation of the Laws of England.* Translated by Francis Grigor. London, 1917, chap. IX, p. 17.

[106]Voegelin, l.c., p. 43.

[107]Ibid.

would be the sacramental bond of the community." This sacramental bond, he says, "would be neither the Logos of Christ ... nor a perverted Logos as it lives in modern totalitarian communities." Nevertheless Fortescue was on the "search for an immanent Logos of society"; "he was not clear about the implications" of his search but "he found a name for it; he called it the *intencio popupli.* This *intencio populi* is the center of the mystical body of the realm; ... he described it as the heart from which is transmitted into the head and members of the body as its nourishing blood stream the political provision for the well-being of the people." But Voegelin emphasizes that "the animating center for a social body is not to be found in any of its human members. The *intencio populi* is located neither in the royal representative nor in the people as a multitude of subjects but is the intangible living center of the realm as a whole. The word 'people' in this formula does not signify an external multitude of human beings but the mystical substance erupting in articulation; and the word 'intention' signifies the urge or drive of this substance to erupt and to maintain itself in articulate existence as an entity which, by means of its articulation can provide for its well-being."[108]

This interpretation gives rise to the impression that Fortescue was a mystic. This, however, is not the case. In his *Commendations of the Laws of England*, to which Voegelin's interpretation refers, Fortescue says expressly to the prince for whom he wrote this work, as a reply to the argument that a kingdom ought to be governed by the best of laws but that "nature always covets what is best": "Sir! there is no such mystery in these things.."[109] Fortescue simply compares the state as a body politic – as so many others have done before and after him – without any metaphysical or mystical intention, with the body of man. The purpose of this comparison is in the first place to show – a point not mentioned by Voegelin – that "it is absolutely necessary, where a company of men combine and form themselves into a *body politic*, that some one should preside as the governing principal, who goes usually under the name of *King*."[110] The decisive argument is: just as the human body must have a head, a state must choose a king. "In this order, as out of an embrio, is formed an human body, with one head to govern and control it; so, from a confused multitude is formed a regular kingdom, which is a sort of a mystical body, with one person, as the head, to guide and govern. And, as in the natural body (according to the *philosopher*) the heart is the first thing which lives, having in it the blood, which it transmits to all the other members, thereby importing life, and growth and vigour; so in the body politic, the first thing which lives and moves is the intention of

[108]L.c., p. 44.
[109]Fortescue, l.c., chapt. VII, p. 13.
[110]L.c., chapt. XIII, p. 21.

the people, having it in the blood, that is the prudential care and provision for the public good, which it transmits and communicates to the head, as the principal part ... "[111] From this passage it follows that Fortescue employs the term "a sort of mystic body" only in order to stress that the political body is not a "natural body", that only a comparison is meant. He uses the term political "body" in no other sense than it is used in ordinary language. As to the meaning of the "intention of the people", his comparison of this element with the heart shows plainly his view of the essential part the people plays in a limited monarchy. What he is driving at in this respect becomes clear by his comparison of the laws of the state with the "nerves or sinews of the body natural ... . And as the head of the body cannot change its nerves or sinews, ... *neither can a king, who is the head of the body politic, change the laws thereof, nor take from the people what is their's, by right*, against their consents"[112] There can be no doubt that "people" means the "company of men" of which he says in the above-quoted passage that they "combine and form themselves into a body politic." What he has in mind when he refers to the people is indicated in one of the most important statements of his political theory, which Voegelin does not quote: "*For he [the king] is appointed to protect his subjects in their lives, properties and laws; for this very end and purpose he has the delegation of power from the people; and has no just claim to any other power but this.*"[113] There is nothing of a "mystical substance erupting in articulation," nothing of a "sacramental bond of the community," nothing of an "immanent Logos"[114] in the people from which the king, according to the theory of Fortescue, derives his power.

The final result of Fortescue's doctrine of representation is – according to Voegelin – the statement: Since "the king is in his realm what the pope is in the church, a *servus servorum Dei*", "all that the king does ought to be referred to his kingdom."[115] Voegelin calls this doctrine "the most concentrated formulation of the problem of representation." We may assume that he considers Fortescue's doctrine as the perfect formulation of the existential, not merely elemental, representation. But the statement that the acts of the king are to be imputed to the kingdom means only that the king is the organ of the state, and the statement that the king is a *servus servorum Dei* nothing but a metaphysical expression of the idea that it is his duty to serve his subjects. The statements are taken from Fortescue, *The Governance of England*, and read as follows: "Wherefore all he doth owith to be referred to his kingdom. For though his estate be the highest estate temporal in the earth,

[111]Ibid.

[112]L.c., chapt. XIII, p. 22.

[113]Ibid.

[114]Voegelin, l.c., pp. 43f.

[115]L.c., p. 45.

yet it is an office, in which the mynestrith to his reaume defence and justice. And therefore he may say of him selff and off his reaum, as the pope saith off him selff and the church, in that he writithe, servus servorum Dei." Consequently the state must financially sustain the king as the church sustains the pope. The statements are made in chapter VIII dealing with the question of the finances of the king. Neither the statement that all the king does ought to be referred to his kingdom, nor the statement that the king is in his realm what the pope is in the church can be regarded as a contribution to the theory of existential representation. Interesting is only the statement which Fortescue makes in his *De laudibus legum Anglie*, and which Voegelin does not quote: that the king "has the delegation of power from the people." For it may be interpreted to mean that the king represents the people although he is not elected, nor can be dismissed by the people, nor are his actions determined by the people. The only basis of the idea that he represents the people is that he is obliged to protect the people and that he cannot change the law against the will of the people represented in Parliament. His government is interpreted as a government by the people only and exclusively because it is a government for, or not against, the people. This, of course, is a fiction. And the purpose of the fiction is not only to emphasize the moral obligation of the king to govern in the interest of the people but also – and not at the least – to strengthen the authority of the king by the idea that he represents the people, that the people governs through him. No government can claim to represent the people or have its power from the people if the establishment of the government is legally independent of the will of its subjects, organized in popular assemblies or electorates. It is the same fiction as used by Soviet political theory which presents communist party dictatorship as a democratic government only because it claims to govern in the interest of the people. Is it the intention of the theory of existential, and not merely elemental, representation to legitimize this fiction?

In order to demonstrate "articulation" as condition of not merely elemental but existential representation, Voegelin goes back to a writer of the 8th century, Paulus Diaconus, author of the *History of the Lombards*. However, this display of profound knowledge of historical literature is hardly in proportion to its result. It is the fact reported by Paulus Dioconus that the Lombards after having been ruled by two dukes, set themselves a king, and, then, "the victorious wars began."[116] The moral of the story – and perhaps of all history – according to Voegelin is: "To be articulate for action meant to have a king; to lose the king meant to lose fitness for action, when the group did not act, it did not need a king."[117] Action, of course, means war. Is it the

[116]L.c., p. 47.
[117]Ibid.

platitude that democracy is not the best form of articulation for the purpose of waging war, that Voegelin wants to prove? Or is it rather the thought, scantily hidden behind the platitude: that an autocratic military leader is in a more profound sense of the term a "representative" of the people than a democratic government, because the former does, whereas the latter does not "articulate" the people for action and thus provides the "desired substance"?

The last source from which Voegelin tries to extricate the idea of an existential and not merely elemental representation is Maurice Hauriou's *Precis de Droit constitutionel.*[118] Hauriou is a typical representative of the traditional theory of public law prevailing in France during the first half of the 20th century. Therefore it would be surprising to find in his writings a new doctrine of representation. Voegelin asserts that according to Hauriou "To be a representative means to guide, in a ruling position, the work of realizing the idea through institutional embodiment, and the power of a ruler has authority in so far as he is able to make his factual power representative of the idea."[119] The "idea" is what Hauriou calls *idée directrice*. By "realizing the idea of the institution" the government becomes "representative in the existential sense", not in the merely "constitutional", that is, "elemental sense."[120] If we examine what Hauriou has to say about representation we find that he uses this term – as do most of the writers on constitutional law and political theory – in different meanings. He distinguishes between the representation of an individual by an individual ("*l'homme qui agit au nom d'un autre homme est son représentant*") and representation of an institution, especially the state, by an individual (*l'homme qui agit au nom d'une institution est également son représentant ou son organe*").[121] He emphasizes that in the field of public law the term "représentant" means the same as "organe"; he says that it is quite impossible to define the organs of a juristic person without making it apparent that they are in some way "representatives."[122] As far as the organs of the state are concerned, he distinguishes them from simple agents or employees ("des simple agents ou commis"). An organ representing the state is characterized by the fact that the individual having this capacity has the power of initiative and is politically responsible.[123] Finally, he uses the term "representation" to designate the specific democratic form of representation. His definition of representative government runs as follows: "The representative government may be defined as a government in which one or two assemblies elected by the people repre-

[118]Maurice Hauriou, *Precis de Droit constitutionel*, 2nd ed., 1929.

[119]Voegelin, l.c., p. 48.

[120]L.c., p. 49.

[121]Hauriou, p. 19.

[122]L.c., p. 209.

[123]L.c., p. 212/13.

sent the people vis-a-vis the central power and participate in the government, first, by voting taxes, then, by voting laws."[124] Hence, "to be a representative" may mean many things quite different from what Voegelin presents as Hauriou's doctrine concerning the meaning of being a representative. The *idée directrice*, which, according to Voegelin plays so important a role in Hauriou's doctrine that Voegelin attributes to its realization the transformation of a merely elemental into an existential representation, is according to Hauriou simply the idea of organization. Examining the problem of social organization from a sociological point of view, Hauriou says in opposition to other doctrines especially the organism theory – that the primary phenomena of social organization are of political character: the coming into existence of a directing or founding center (*centre directeur ou fondateur*) of governmental organs, governmental equilibrium, and, finally consentments. "The role of the directing or founding center is to implant an idea in the social milieu; this idea is that of the organization to be created, considered as an enterprise to be realized; it implies a plan of the organization and, consequently, contains potentially the form of the latter."[125] This idea is the *idée directrice.* "A social organization," says Hauriou, "becomes durable ... when, owing to the balance of organs and power, "the government can be subordinated to the *idée directrice* which is within the organization from the moment of its foundation, and when this system of ideas and balance of powers has been confirmed, in its form, by the consentment of the members of the institution as well as the social millieu."[126] The theory that a social organization comes into existence when its idea is implanted in the social milieu is highly problematical, and the statements concerning the durability of social organizations are truisms. Neither the one nor the other is in essential connection with Hauriou's doctrine of representation, which does not deviate in any respect from the traditional view. There is nothing in this doctrine from which the "lesson" could be drawn which Voegelin formulates as the result of his analysis: "In order to be representative, it is not enough for a government to be representative in a constitutional sense (our elemental type of representative institutions); it must also be representative in the existential sense of realizing the idea of the institution."[127] Hauriou's above-quoted definition of representative government shows not the slightest tendency toward Voegelin's existentialism. And there is no basis of Voegelin's assertion that Hauriou's theory of representation implies the "warning ...: If a government is nothing but representative in the constitutional sense a representative ruler

[124]L.c., p. 147.
[125]L.c., p. 72.
[126]L.c., p. 73.
[127]Voegelin, l.c., p. 49.

in the existential sense will sooner or later make an end of it; and quite possible the new existential ruler will not be too representative in the constitutional sense."[128] It is not Hauriou, it is the new science of politics which conveys this warning, the meaning of which can only be an appeal for a political reform by which the merely elemental representation, that is, the democratic form of government, is transformed into a regime capable of organizing the mass of the people into a body fit for action.

2.2.2 2.

After having dealt under the – not quite appropriate – heading "representation and existence" with the problem of representation of the state by its organs, Voegelin pretends to deal with another aspect of the problem of representation under the heading "representation and truth." But the topic treated in this chapter has nothing to do with the representation of the state by its organs and even less with the problem of truth.

The social phenomenon to which Voegelin calls the attention of the reader is the well known fact that at a relatively primitive state of social and intellectual evolution the social order is interpreted as being in conformity with a divine will, the will of the gods or of a special god, or of a god supposed to be the only existing God. A characteristic version of this interpretation is the idea that the social order, especially the legal order of a state, is the imitation of the order of the universe, a microcosm, a little world as the image of the macrocosm, the big world. It is a theological ideology of society and a typical attempt at presenting the given social order as the realization of divine justice on earth. Its purpose is obviously to justify this order and thus to confirm and strengthen the authority of the ruler, who – this is the most important part of this ideology – is presented as a descendant or deputy of God. If the alleged relationship between the divine order of the world and the social order in question is termed "representation," if one says, as Voegelin does, that according to this idea the social order "represents" the divine order of the cosmos, the term representation has a totally different meaning than when it is used to express the relationship of the state to its organs. Representation in this case means organship, representation in the other case means likeness, image picture, reproduction, and the like. These, by the way, are not the only meanings of the term, which, e.g., is used also to designate a dramatic production or performance. Under the cover of this term with many different meanings, Voegelin treats two totally different problems which have nothing to do with each other, claiming that the analysis of the one adds something to the understanding of the other.

[128] Ibid.

The interpretation of an established social order as being in conformity with the divine order of the world is not primarily a self-interpretation of society, as Voegelin asserts. It is the result of religious speculation by priests, a theological theory of society. It is quite understandable that this theological theory is adopted by the ruler of the state, in whose interests the ideology evidently is elaborated, and thus becomes secondarily a self-interpretation of society. It is a typical case where the symbols of self-interpretation of society cannot be separated from theoretical concepts. But Voegelin speaks of these ideologies as of "symbols in which a society interprets the meaning of its existence ... "[129]

More serious, because utterly misleading, is the interpretation of the ideology in question as "representation of truth." Voegelin asserts that the meaning of the ideology according to which a state order is the imitation of the divine order of the cosmos is that society interprets itself as the "representation of truth"[130]; and the new science of politics accepts this interpretation. Voegelin confronts the "truth represented by society" with the "truth represented by the theorist" which is the truth of the statements a social theorist makes about society. In the phrase "representation of a truth by a theorist" the term representation has a third meaning, different from that which it has in the phrases "representation of a state by its organ" and "representation of the divine order by the state order." Voegelin raises the question: "If the truth represented by the theorist should be different from the truth represented by society, how can the one be developed out of the other by something that looks as innocuous as a critical clarification?"[131] That shows that Voegelin considers the truth represented by society as being of the same kind as the truth claimed by a scientific statement. He refers to the case where a "truth represented by the theorist was opposed to another truth represented by society," and asks: "is such language empty, or is there really something like a representation of truth to be found in political societies in history?" It is of the greatest importance to note that Voegelin does not formulate the problem which he calls "representation of truth" as the problem of a political ideology falsely pretending to express a truth, but as the question whether there is "really something like a representation of truth to be found." He presupposes an affirmative answer to this question. He insists upon the view that the problem of representation is not exhausted "by representation in the existential sense," that it is "necessary to distinguish between representation of society by its articulated representatives and a second relation in which society itself becomes the representative of something beyond itself, of a

---

[129]L.c., p. 53.
[130]Ibid.
[131]Ibid.

transcendent reality."[132] This transcendent reality is the truth "represented" by society. And because this truth is "truth" in the specific sense of the term, in the same sense as the truth of a scientific statement, truth in a logical and epistemological sense, Voegelin is dealing with an ideology according to which a social order is the imitation of the cosmic order.

It may be that theological ideologists, and rulers adopting the ideologies produced by these ideologists working in the service of the rulers, speak of a divine truth, realized in a society constituted by a given social order. But what they mean by this truth is not a truth in the logical and epistemological sense, not a truth of science, but a moral-political value: justice. The confusion of truth with justice is a characteristic element of unscientific, religious speculation. Truth in a scientific sense is the quality of a proposition, and a proposition is true if it is in conformity with reality; justice is the quality of human behavior or of a normative order established by acts of human behavior. It means conformity with a supreme norm presupposed to be valid. If, as it is assumed in theological speculation, reality is created by the will of God, who is absolutely just, and hence justice is immanent in reality, truth and justice seem to coincide. When Jesus stands before Pilatus, the Gospel of St. John – essentially influenced by theological speculations – lets him say: "I was born to bear witness to the truth. Every one who is of the truth hears my voice." But what he meant was: he was born to bear witness to justice, the justice that he was about to establish in the kingdom of God, this realization of divine justice on earth; or – as Voegelin, confirming the language of the Gospel without an attempt at "critical clarification", would say, – the representation of a transcendent truth.

As an example of a "cosmological empire", that is to say, a state which by its theological ideologists and, then, by its rulers has been interpreted as the representation of truth, Voegelin refers to Persia under Achaemenides. He quotes an inscription "celebrating the feats of Darius I," according to which "the king was victorious because he was the righteous tool of Ahuramazda; he 'was not wicked, nor a liar'; neither he nor his family were servants of Ahriman, of the Lie, but 'ruled according to righteousness.' "[133] It is evident that here truth means the same as righteousness; that is, justice. And if the enemies of the king are called liars, if it is said that "lies made them revolt," nothing else is expressed but the judgment of the king that revolution is a crime, because against justice. The new science of politics, accepting without objection this confusion of truth with justice, considers the king as the representative of the truth and the revolutionaries as "representatives of the Lie". The inscription contains the passage: "By the grace of Ahuramazda

[132]L.c., p. 54.
[133]L.c., p. 55.

there is also much else that has been done by me which is not graven in this inscription; it has not been inscribed lest he who should read this inscription hereafter should then hold that which has been done by me to be too much and should not believe it, but should take it to be lies."[134] This means – expressed in a typical oriental exaggeration: the deeds of the king are incredibly great. But Voegelin's interpretation is: "No fibs for a representative of the truth; he must even lean over backward."[135]

Another "cosmic" empire, that is, a state that interprets itself as representative of a transcendent truth – the truth which the new political science tries to find in political societies in history – is the empire of the Mongols. To prove the cosmic character of this empire Voegelin quotes some passages from a letter of the ruler of the Mongols to the Pope in which the former rejects the request of the latter that the Mongols should receive baptism and submit to the authority of the Church. In the letter the Khan of the Mongols asserts, as dozens of other kings of much smaller kingdoms have asserted and still assert, that he has his authority from his God: "By the virtue of God, from the rising of the sun to its setting, all realms have been granted to us"; and of course, that his god is the true god: "By order of the living God Genghis Khan, the sweet and venerable Son of God, says: God is high above all, He, Himself, the immortal God, and on earth, Genghis Khan is the only Lord."[136] If such a statement is sufficient for the science of politics to interpret the realm of the Mongols as representation of truth, it was not necessary to go back as far as that in history. The Kingdom of Prussia under William II., who again and again asserted to be by the grace of God the ruler of men, or modern Japan the emperor of which is worshiped as a son of God, were as good examples of cosmic empires and representation of truth as the Mongol empire. If a political science has to say about this ideology anything else but that it is a lie spread by agents of the respective governments for the purpose of bolstering their authority, it exposes itself to the suspicion of having purposes other than that to bear witness to the truth. Plato, to be sure, whose metaphysics the new science considers as its foundation, has another idea of truth. He distinguishes not only between truth and lies but also between two kinds of lies: lies which are and lies which are not politically useful. If they are politically useful, the government – but only the government – is allowed to use them. They are a kind of truth, a political truth. But taking a lie, for political reasons, as a truth, is the typical device of an illusive ideology. It has no place in a scientific description of political reality.

If the Khan of the Mongols who rejects baptism and submission to the

---

[134]L.c., pp. 55f.

[135]L.c., p. 56.

[136]L.c., pp. 57, 58.

authority of the Pope is a representative of truth because he asserts himself to be the son of God, then the Pope, who asserts to be the deputy of God on earth, is also a representative of truth, and, hence, there exists "a conflict of truth," a situation which Voegelin seriously considers to be possible. But if "truth" is taken in its scientific, and not in its political sense, no conflict of truth is possible, because of two contradictory statements only one can be true, the other being rejected as untrue. This is especially the case to which Voegelin refers when he speaks of a conflict of truth. It is the case where "a truth represented by the theorist was opposed to another truth represented by society."[137] If what the theorist asserts is true, and, is opposed to the self-interpretation of society, then this self-interpretation is not "another truth", but a lie. It is another truth only in the Platonic sense according to which a lie, if it is useful to the government, is a truth. If a lie can be a truth, no "critical clarification" of the self-interpretation of society – a task of political science recognized by Voegelin – is possible.

Critical clarification of self-interpretation of society is just that function of a social science which is called critique of ideology. It is self-evident that the new science of politics cannot renounce this function. Hence Voegelin is looking for a truth "that is apt to challenge the truth of the cosmological empires."[138] Why only the truth of the cosmological empires, why not the truth of any self-interpretation of society – or social ideology – is not quite understandable. For the truth "apt to challenge the truth of the cosmological empires" must be apt to challenge any truth which is challengeable, and that means which is not as it pretends to be a truth, but a lie. It can be only the truth of science. This truth is not a secret treasure hidden somewhere to be discovered by a visionary, but is a rational method, the result of the development of science in general and social science in particular. It can by its very nature, not be the exclusive possession of a particular school of thought. But according to Voegelin's new science of politics, there is a "discovery" of this truth, and this discovery is "a historical event of major dimensions."[139] Which is this historical event?

The discovery of the truth, Voegelin asserts, has taken place roughly in "the period from 800 to 300 B.C.", and occurred "simultaneously in the various civilizations but without apparent mutual influence"; in China, India, Persia, Israel, and Hellas. The discoverers of the truth are Confucius and Lao-tse, the writers of the *Upanishads* and Buddha, Zoroaster, the Jewish prophets, some philosophers and poets of ancient Greece. Hence it is in religious speculations, that is just there where the truth of the cosmological

---

[137]L.c., p. 53.
[138]L.c., p. 60.
[139]Ibid.

empires, the truths of the self-interpretation of societies have their origin, that the truth is to be found by which these self-interpretations are to be challenged. How the truth of which Darius I. pretended to be the representative by asserting that he was victorious "because he was the righteous tool of Ahuramazda" and not a servant of Ahriman, could be "challenged" by the truth discovered by Zoroaster, who founded the religion of Ahura Mazda and Ahriman which is the source of King Darius' truth, is indiscoverable. And even more mysterious is how it is possible to find one and the same truth in religions which are so different as that of Zoroaster and that of the Jewish prophets, or between the thought of the Buddha and the doctrine of ideas of Plato; or even between the ethics of Confucius, which did not refer to a particular god, and the metaphysics of Aristotle, which backed the polytheistic religion of Greece. Voegelin speaks of a "simultaneous outbreak of the truth of the mystic philosophers and prophets"[140]. But if it was an "outbreak" at all, and not the result of gradual evolutions, it was the outbreak of very different truths, and insofar as it was a "mystic" truth, it is hardly apt to challenge the truth of the cosmological empires, or any similar "truths," as a "theoretical truth"[141], "opposed to another truth represented by society"[142]. And it is just for the purpose to find a basis for the opposition of a theoretical interpretation of society to the self-interpretation of society that Voegelin is directing the new political science toward the truth of mystic philosophers.

The difficulty of explaining how so many and partly contradictory truths are to be considered as "the" truth does not exist for Voegelin. For, after having referred to at least five totally different religious and philosophical systems as the sources of the truth for which the new political science is looking, he resolutely restricts the field of the search for this truth by turning "to the more special form which this outbreak, the outbreak of the truth, has assumed in the West." He justifies this restriction by the fact that "only in the West ... has the outbreak culminated in the establishment of philosophy in the Greek sense and in particular of a theory of politics."[143] But why is only philosophy in the Greek sense, and not philosophy or religion, in the Chinese, Indian, Persian, Jewish sense exemplary for the new political science, if the representatives of these philosophies and religions are likewise in the possession of "the" truth, apt to challenge the "truth" of a self-interpretation of society? Why should Greek philosophy, and not Persian religion be used to challenge the truth of the Persian empire, if this truth, too, is an object of the new science of politics? And, above all: why is philosophy in the Greek

[140]Ibid.

[141]Ibid.

[142]L.c., p. 53.

[143]L.c., p. 61.

sense only the metaphysics of Plato and Aristotle and not the philosophy of the Sophists, of Leucippus and Democritus, the founders of the theory of atoms?

That the new science of politics has no answer to these questions could be forgiven as a pardonable sin, if it only would answer that question which is decisive in its fight against positivism because this answer alone could justify its claim to substitute for a destructive pseudo-science a constructive, true science of politics. It is the answer to the question: What is this "challenging theoretical truth"[144] which Voegelin promises to disclose when he says that its establishment is "a rather complex affair requiring a more detailed examination."[145]

It has been pointed out that Voegelin considers himself entitled to restrict these examinations to "philosophy in the Greek sense." First, he examines Plato's formula "that a polis is man written large."[146] Voegelin does not mention the decisive point: that Plato uses this analogy between man and state only in order to answer the question, what is justice, as a virtue of man. The result at which Plato aims with this analogy is that justice is achieved when in the soul of man the rational element (reason) rules over the emotional elements (feelings and will). The postulate to act reasonably is a commonplace and in itself no answer to the question of justice. But Plato uses this empty formula in order to justify his postulate that in the ideal state a small group of so-called philosophers shall rule – with the help of the army (the warriors) as their instrument – over the working people, completely excluded from any direct or indirect participation in the government. This extremely autocratic regime is the just order of the ideal state, presented by Plato not as a definite, only as a provisional answer to the question of justice; but it is the only answer we can find in his *Republic*. There is no reference to the constitution of the ideal state in Voegelin's analysis of Plato's analogy between man and state.

Voegelin formulates the result of his analysis as follows: "Plato was engaged concretely in the exploration of the human soul, and the true order of the soul turned out to be dependent on philosophy in the strict sense of the love of the divine *sophon*."[147] *Sophon* means wisdom. What wisdom? Wisdom in general or a special wisdom? And what is the truth thus achieved? Voegelin continues: "The true order of man, thus, is a constitution of the soul, to be defined in terms of certain experiences which have become predominant to the point of forming a character. The true order of the soul in

[144]L.c., p. 60.
[145]L.c., p. 60.
[146]L.c., p. 61.
[147]L.c., p. 63.

this sense furnishes the standard for measuring and classifying the empirical variety of human types as well as of the social order in which they find their expression." But which is the "true" and that means according to Plato, the just – "order of the soul"? Without a precise determination of the constitution, no standard of measuring social orders is possible. Why does Voegelin not reproduce Plato's answer to this question, why does he not say, that – according to Plato – the only just order of the state is the autocratic constitution of his ideal republic?

Voegelin proceeds to Aristotle's Ethics, which, as is well-known, is an ethics of virtues. The question as to what is morally good, which are the norms of the moral order, is answered by the enumeration of certain virtues, such as courage, truthfulness, and the like. Again, Voegelin does not mention the essential point of the Aristotelian ethics, the principle according to which the question can be answered: How to define the virtues a man must have in order to be considered as morally good. It is the famous doctrine that in ethics virtue can be defined just as in geometry the point dividing a given line into two equal parts can be determined. For virtue is the middle between two extremes, which are vices. This is the so called *mesotes* doctrine (*mesos* meaning the middle). Sine the extremes, i.e., the vices, must be known in order to find out what is between them, just as the two endpoints of a line must be given in order to determine the center, Aristotle's ethics presupposes as self-evident what is to be considered as a vice; and since a vice implies – as its opposite – the virtue, the ethics of Aristotle amounts to a systematization of the traditional morals of Greece at his time. This is Aristotle's positive contribution to the science of ethics.[148] But there is not a word of this in Voegelin's analysis of Aristotle's ethics. He only gives a "brief catalogue" of certain virtues, namely, "love of the *sophon*," that is, love of wisdom; "the variants of the Platonic Eros toward the *kalon* and the *agathon*", that is, the desire for the beautiful and the good; "the Platonic Dike," that is, justice; the "right superordination and subordination of the forces in the soul,"; "and, above all, ... the experience of death, as the cathartic experience of the soul which purifies conduct by placing it ... into the perspective of death."[149] Yet the virtues to love wisdom, the beautiful and the good and justice, and to place conduct into the perspective of death are insignificant generalities as long as we do not learn what is the content of wisdom, what is beautiful, good, just, which conduct should be placed in the perspective of death, and what is the result of such placing. These are the questions to be answered by a political science which pretends to be in the possession of the "truth." What Voegelin has to say in this respect is not an answer to these questions.

[148]Cf. Kelsen, "Metamorphoses of the Idea of Justice", pp. 190ff.

[149]Voegelin, l.c., p. 65.

He does not convey even "brief and incomplete ... hints", as he modestly asserts.[150] He presents nothing but a catalogue of questions.

After having asserted that the truth of the soul according to Plato can be achieved through the love of wisdom, without telling us anything about this wisdom, and leaving us completely in the dark about the content of this truth of the soul, Voegelin increases the mystery by the statement: "The discovery of the new truth [which is the truth of the soul] is not [– as it could be assumed –] an advancement of psychological knowledge in the – immanent sense." If psychology, the science, the object of which is the soul, cannot describe the truth of the soul, the suspicion arises that it is not at all the soul the truth of which is in question. But Voegelin is still dealing only with the soul. The truth of the soul, he says, cannot be discovered by psychology: "One would rather have to say that the psyche" – for some unknown reason he calls the soul now by its Greek form – "itself is found as a new center in man at which he experiences himself as open toward transcendental reality."[151] An empirical science like psychology cannot find in the soul an open door through which "transcendental reality" may enter. Such discovery is denied to any science, but reserved to the metaphysics of mystic philosophers.

"The psyche as the region in which transcendence is experienced must be differentiated out of a more compact structure of the soul, ... " Then comes the tautological statement: "the openness of the soul is experienced through the opening of the soul itself"; and, finally, the admission: "This opening, which is as much action as it is passion, we owe to the genius of the mystic philosophers."[152] The new political science thus enters the nebulous region of mysticism. Since there are many men – and among them certainly many political scientists – who will confess that they never experienced themselves as open toward transcendent reality, and since Voegelin is of the opinion that this experience is essential with respect to that truth toward which the new political science is to be orientated, he must describe this experience, must tell us what he knows about the object of that experience, namely, the transcendental reality. As long as, for some reason or another, he does not comply with this requirement, he cannot expect that his statement about the truth of the soul is considered as anything but a meaningless agglomeration of words. And he has indeed not the slightest intention to satisfy our curiosity. Instead he adds to the mysterious "truth of the soul" a new, even more mysterious truth, which evidently is the truth at which the new science is aiming. He says: "Through the opening of the soul the philosopher finds himself in

[150] L.c., p. 66.
[151] L.c., p. 67.
[152] Ibid.

a new relation with God; he not only discovers his own psyche as the instrument for experiencing transcendence but at the same time discovers the divinity in its radically nonhuman transcendence. Hence, the differentiation of the psyche is inseparable from a new truth about God."[153] If somebody boasts of having found a new truth he has to show the difference which exists between the new and the old truth. Voegelin of course is not in a position to show this difference because he knows as little about the new as he knows about the old "truth of God." If the truth of God is the truth of the new political science, then this science is theology, and that means the hopeless attempt to achieve human knowledge of something which, by definition, is not accessible to human knowledge. Besides, if theology is a science at all, it is certainly not a "new" science, and Voegelin's effort to establish it is completely superfluous. He has the choice among a remarkable number of quite different theologies, of which each claims to have its own "truth of God." And, indeed, the truth of God in Plato's theology is quite different from the truth of God in the protestant or the catholic theologies. If Voegelin demands that political science turn to theology, he has to say precisely which theology he has in mind, or, what amounts to the same, he has to indicate the God whose truth the new science of politics should accept. Is it really the God of Plato? What about the theology of Thomas Aquinas, for whom Voegelin, in the Introduction to his book, showed almost the same enthusiasm as for Plato? Catholic theologians – certainly more competent in this respect than a professor of political science – will probably not recognize the speculation of a heathen philosopher about the impersonal idea of the agathon as the truth of the God of the Bible.

The result of Voegelin's examination concerning the "theoretical truth" with the aid of which the new science of politics has to fulfill its task: to challenge the truth of the self-interpretation of society or – to formulate this task in the usual way – to perform a critique of social ideologies, are the statements that there exists a truth of the soul and a truth of God, and that the one is connected with the other. By these statements nothing more is affirmed than that there exists a God and that the soul is able to achieve some experience of God. Even if these unproved and unprovable statements are accepted, they are of no use at all to a political science which – as Voegelin postulates – has to solve the problems of social values, that is to say, has to decide the questions as to whether democracy or autocracy is the best form of government, capitalism or communism the best economic organization, pacifism or imperialism, nationalism or internationalism the best policy. No value judgment concerning social institutions or political actions can properly be deduced from these completely empty statements. It seems that

[153] Ibid.

Voegelin anticipated this objection. For he says: "The theorist is the representative of a new truth in rivalry with the truth represented by society. So much is secured. But there seems to be left the difficulty of the impasse that the new truth has little chance of becoming socially effective, of forming a society in its image."[154] Indeed, how could a society be formed in the image of a truth the content of which is unknown? But Voegelin immediately adds: "This impasse, in fact, did never exist." We may expect that now Voegelin will show how a society can be formed in the image of the truth of God in connection with the truth of the soul, in spite of the fact that the content of these truths remains unknown. In order to avoid any uncertainty about the status of the problem, we have to remember that when Voegelin refers to the truth of the soul and the truth of God as signposts for the new science of politics he does not refer to the constitution of Plato's ideal state or Aristotle's political suggestions. As pointed out, he does not even mention the former and takes only Aristotle's ethics of virtues into consideration. The problem, as he formulates it, is a problem of "the theorist" – that is, political scientist –, as "the representative of a new truth,"[155] i.e., the truth of the soul and of God, facing the truth represented by society – any society whatsoever –; it is the problem of "forming society" – any society whatsoever, not only Greek society – in the image of the truth of the soul and the truth of God, and not in the image of a concrete political program developed by Plato or Aristotle or any other of the mystic philosophers or prophets to whom he attributes the discovery of "the challenging theoretical truth."

The way in which Voegelin tries to convince the reader that a society can be formed in conformity with the empty formulas "truth of the soul" and "truth of God" is, indeed, more than astonishing. He refers to "the Athens of Marathon and the tragedy" and says: "Here, for a golden hour in history, the miracle had happened of a political society articulated down to the individual citizen as a representable unit, the miracle of a generation which individually experienced the responsibility of representing the truth of the soul and expressed this experience through the tragedy as a public cult."[156] In the battle of Marathon the Athenian Army distinguished itself by a heroic attitude. This is the historic fact on which Voegelin bases his interpretation, that the Athenian society represented at that time the truth of the soul. But until now, he had not told us that the truth of the soul or the truth of God means the moral norm prescribing an heroic attitude in war. His statement that at the time of the battle of Marathon the state of Athens was "a political society articulated down to the individual citizen as a representable unit which indi-

[154]L.c., p. 70.
[155]Ibid.
[156]L.c., p. 71.

vidually experienced the responsibility of representing the truth of the soul" is without any foundation if it means more than that in the battle of Marathon the Athenian army exhibited an heroic attitude. No accumulation of poetical phrases like the "golden hour in history" or the "miracle of a generation" can make the critical reader forget that behind all these words there is nothing but the fact of a heroically fought battle, as has been fought by many other armies of many other nations, and that, if valiant fighting is sufficient for a political science to interpret the society concerned as a representative of the soul, this interpretation does not add anything essential to the statement that the army of that society distinguished itself in a heroic battle. But it is rather significant that Voegelin's truth of the soul when it assumes some concrete content refers to militaristic ideals, just as his concept of existential representation refers, if not exclusively then primarily, to warlike action.

In order to demonstrate that the Athenian society – at least for a short time – represented the truth of the soul, Voegelin presents an analysis of Aeschylus' tragedy the *Suppliants*. In this drama the highly religiously-minded poet tried to show that in a conflict between positive law and the natural or divine law, i.e., the Dike of Zeus, the latter prevails. As usual in Greek tragedy, the chorus expresses the moral of the play: "It is Zeus who brings the end to pass." The purpose of the play is – as that of many other plays of Aeschylus and Sophocles – to strengthen the belief in the religion of the state and thus authority of the government, using religion as one of its most effective instruments. This is, from the point of a political science which considers as its task a critique of ideology, the significance of this as of many other Greek tragedies. But what is, according to the new science of politics presented by Voegelin, the political importance of the *Suppliants*? The fact that the king in the play decides to apply the divine law is interpreted to mean: "the royal descent into the depth of the soul" and that this "decision represents the truth of the God."[157] But this decision of the king does not root deeper in his soul than any other decision; and if it "represents" anything divine, it does not represent the truth, but the justice of God, "the Dike of Zeus," as Voegelin himself asserts. This is exactly the idea expressed in the tragedy; and if, as Voegelin emphasizes, the "tragedy was a public cult," this interpretation of the tragedy is also a self-interpretation of society. The new political science does not at all challenge this self-interpretation, it does not denounce the tragedy as a political ideology. On the contrary, it takes over this ideologically self-interpretation without any critique.

By referring to the play of Aeschylus, Voegelin wants to show – as he expressly declares – that the tragedy intended to make the people "understand the Athenian *prostasia* as the organization of a people under a leader

[157] L.c., p. 73.

– in which the leader tries to represent the Jovian Dike and uses his power of persuasion to create the same state of the soul in the people on occasion of concrete decisions, while the people are willing to follow such persuasive leadership into the representation of truth ... "[158] That means that the tragedy tried to strengthen the belief of the people in Zeus and the other gods of the Greek religion and in the authority of their leaders as the executives of the will of the gods. But if a political science, as the new science of politics, approves of this ideological function of the tragedy, and by approving it presents itself as the representative of a truth of God, it proves to be itself a political ideology. Voegelin refers to the *Suppliants* of Aeschylus, a pro-religious play, as representative of the Greek tragedy. But only the tragedies of Aeschylus and Sophocles have the tendency to support the state religion as an instrument of the state policy. The plays of the third great poet, Euripides, assumed a highly critical attitude toward religion. Euripides, the poet of the Greek enlightenment, is as much a representative of the Greek tragedy as the conservative Aeschylus. It is significant that Voegelin ignores completely this aspect of the Greek tragedy, just as he ignores the intellectual movement of the sophists, against which Plato's philosophy was the reaction. He mentions only the *Troades* of Euripides and this only to say that "the issue is the mass of filth, abuse, vulgarity and atrocity displayed by the Greeks on occasion of the fall of Troy."[159] By referring only to the issue of this play, Voegelin does not do justice to the great political importance of the work of Euripides.

The fact that a head of a state, like Darius or a Mongol Khan, pretends to realize the will of a god is no sufficient reason for a political science to interpret this state – as Voegelin does – as a "cosmological" empire representing a "truth". It stands to reason that the battle of Marathon is no proof of the assertion that the Athenian society, even only temporarily, was the representation of the truth of the soul and that the Greek tragedy is no proof of the assertion that the Athenian society was at any time the representation of the truth of God. But Voegelin seriously affirms to have shown that "society as a whole proved to represent a transcendent truth."[160] A critical analysis of his attempt to demonstrate this thesis can not help revealing the complete lack of foundation.

---

[158] Ibid.

[159] L.c., p. 74.

[160] L.c., p. 76.

2.2.3 3.

Under the heading "the struggle for representation in the Roman empire," Voegelin is dealing in the main, with four quite different topics: the "beginnings of a theocratic conception of rulership"[161]; the contrast between the doctrine of Varro that the gods were instituted by political society, and the philosophy of Cicero, backing the traditional view that the auspices of Romulus and the rites of Numa laid the foundations of the state, that is to say, the contrast between a religious ideology and an attempt at a critical theory; the transformation of republican Rome into a monarchical empire; and the change from the old polytheistic religion of ancient Rome to Christianity as the state religion of the later empire. All these problems – as we shall see – have nothing to do with the theory of representation as the relationship of the state to its organs, and very little connection with one another.

As an introduction to the discussion of these subjects, Voegelin displays remarkable knowledge of theological problems, such as "*philia* [friendship] between God and men",[162] and the revelation of God's grace "through the incarnation of the Logos in Christ,"[163] He presents his view concerning the "substance of history" which, as he asserts, "consists in the experience in which man gains the understanding of his humanity and together with it the understanding of its limits," and which "entails consequences for a theory of human existence in society which, under the pressure of a secularized civilization, even philosophers of rank sometimes hesitate to accept without reservation."[164] He formulates one of these consequences "as the principle that a theory of human existence in society must operate within the medium of experiences which have differentiated historically." And, applying this principle, he arrives at the conclusion: "Since the maximum of differentiation was achieved through Greek philosophy and Christianity, this means concretely that theory is bound to move within the historical horizon of classic and Christian experiences."[165] One can only hope that Voegelin means by "theory" only political theory and thus does not include natural sciences in his prohibition against going beyond Plato and St. Thomas Aquinas.

To argue against the highly problematical pronunciamentos of Voegelin's theology and theological philosophy of history is superfluous, because they have nothing to do with his treatment of the problems mentioned above.

In order to show the beginnings of a theocratic conception of rulership, Voegelin quite arbitrarily picks out a historic event of minor importance

[161] L.c., p. 85.
[162] L.c., p. 77.
[163] L.c., p. 78.
[164] L.c., pp. 78, 79.
[165] Ibid.

known only to specialists of Byzantine history, but dealt with in a recently published monograph[166]: the affair of the Roman goddess Victoria, in 384. The restoration of this altar was disputed between pagans and the Christian party, and in the course of this dispute St. Ambrose, speaker of the Christian party, used as an argument against the restoration the following sentence: "While all men who are subject to Roman rule serve (*militare*) you emperors and princes of the earth, you yourselves serve (*militare*) the omnipotent God and holy faith."[167] This sentences Voegelin interprets to mean: "The truth of Christ cannot be represented by the *imperium mundi* but only by the service of God."[168] It is easy to show that this is a misinterpretation. The sentence in question is a commonplace in Christian political theory. It expresses nothing but the idea that, just as the citizens are subject to their ruler and obliged to obey his orders, so the ruler is subject to God and obliged to obey his orders. It is the ordinary interpretation of the relation between the ruler and his subjects as a relationship of superordination and subordination. As men "serve" the rulers, the ruler "serves" God; to "serve" means to be subjected. There is a correlation between serving and ruling. The relationship of serving and ruling is a relationship different from the one which is characterized as "representation", that is, the relationship between organ and community. The recognition of the ruler as a servant of God is the Christian justification of his rulership, and has exactly the same ideological function as the formula of the Mongol Khan who presented himself as the Son of God, although it is not the service-relationship, but the father-son relationship which is used for the purpose of justification. Hence Voegelin is wrong when he says that the formula of Ambrose is the inversion of the Mongol formula, because the "formulation of St. Ambrose does not justify the imperial monarchy ... . It does not speak of any rule at all but of service." But it speaks decidedly of the "Roman rule", and "service" is only one side of the relationship of which the other is ruling. Voegelin asserts: "The appeal of St. Ambrose does not go to the imperial ruler but to the Christian who happens to be the incumbent of the office."[169] This is an open contradiction to the wording of St. Ambrose's appeal which is addressed to the ruler of the Roman empire, to the Christian individual in his capacity as ruler of men. That this individual as a Christian is subjected to God would be of no importance at all if this individual were not the emperor and consequently had the power to forbid the restoration of the Altar of Victoria.

[166]Hendrik Berkhof: *Kirche und Kaiser: Eine Untersuchung der Entstehung der byzantinischen und der theokratischen Staatsauffassung im vierten Jahrhundert*, trans. Gottfried W. Locher (Zollikon-Zürich, 1947).

[167]Voegelin, l.c., pp. 84f.

[168]L.c., p. 85.

[169]Ibid.

If the statement that something, especially a community, "represents" the truth of Christ has any meaning at all, it can only mean that the order of the community is in conformity with the prescriptions of the Christian religion. If the emperor serves the Christian God, the empire which is under his rule is in conformity with the prescriptions of the Christian religion. It is the very meaning of St. Ambrose's appeal that the *imperium mundi*, that is, the Roman empire, should be in correspondence with the prescriptions of the Christian religion, or, to use the terminology of Voegelin, should represent the truth of Christ. There is nothing in the sentence of St. Ambrose that could justify Voegelin's interpretation that "the truth of Christ cannot be represented by the *imperium mundi*";[170] and even less foundation for the interpretation that the truth of Christ can be represented "only by the service of God."[171] The representation to which Voegelin refers when he speaks of representation of truth, is representation of truth by a community in the sense he refers to the cosmological empires of the Persians and Mongols as representatives of truth. It is always a "society" which he interprets as the representative of a transcendent truth.[172] How, then, can the service of God represent the truth of Christ? Only if by the service of God Voegelin means the Christian church, the Christian priesthood. There is, of course, no reference to the church in St. Ambrose's sentence. How, then, can Voegelin interpret the sentence as the "beginnings of a theocratic conception of rulership", since theocracy means the rule by priesthood? The answer is clear: By using the term theocracy, well established in political science, to express something that has nothing to do with it. He says: "These are the beginnings of a theocratic conception of rulership in the strict sense, theocracy not meaning a rule by the priesthood but the recognition by the ruler of the truth of God."[173] According to this definition of theocracy a state is a theocracy if the ruler recognizes the truth of God. The ruler recognizes the truth of God if he "serves the omnipotent God and holy faith", as St. Ambrose bids the emperor; and if the emperor does serve the Christian God and the Christian faith, the truth of Christ is indeed represented by the service of God, performed by the emperor representing the *imperium* and, hence, by the *imperium*. If the truth of Christ is not represented by the church, it can be represented only by that society which is called the state, especially when the service of God is to be performed by the head of the state. By his new definition of theocracy, Voegelin disowns his interpretation of St. Ambrose's sentence.

---

[170]Ibid.

[171]Ibid.

[172]Cf. l.c., p. 76.

[173]L.c., pp. 85f.

To date the beginnings of a theocratic conception of rulership – meaning the recognition by the ruler of the truth of God – with the insignificant statement made by a saint, but not exceptionally learned theologian, on occasion of a not very important event in Byzantine history, is strange enough. But even stranger is the fact that Voegelin sees the theocratic conception of rulership "unfolded fully" in the statement made by St. Augustine in his *Civitas Dei*: "the true happiness of the emperor can be measured only by his conduct as a Christian on the throne."[174] This statement is evidently an application of Plato's thesis that only a just man is happy. For St. Augustine identifies justice with Christianity, which identification is one of the characteristic features of the political theory developed in the *Civitas Dei*. St. Augustine's statement has as little to do with a theocratic concept of rulership as the sentence of St. Ambrose.

The second topic treated in the chapter on the struggle for representation in the Roman Empire is the contrast between Varro's and Cicero's attitudes toward the Roman religion. According to Augustine, Varro advocated the view that "the gods were instituted by political society"[175]: which, naturally, Augustine could not accept. Varro's conception is similar to a doctrine advocated by the sophists and rejected by Plato because of its effect of undermining the authority of the established religion, the maintenance of which was an important concern of Plato's political theory. The same tendency prevails in Cicero's philosophy. Cicero accepted the official opinion that the auspices of Romulus and the rites of Numa laid the foundations of the state (in the words of Voegelin).[176] The opposition between the Varronic and the Ciceronian conception is the old conflict between a rationalistic critical and an anti-rationalistic dogmatic, hence, politically conservative attitude toward religion as an ideology of the state. Voegelin asserts: "The Varronic and Ciceronian expositions are precious documents for the theorist."[177] The theorist can find in the conflict between Plato and the sophists much more material concerning the opposition between a pro-religious and an anti-religious political theory. But since Voegelin is interested here in Roman history, the antagonism between Roman authors may be of more importance than a conflict in the intellectual history of Greece. Granted this, why does Voegelin consider the conflict so "precious" for the theorist? Because he wants to show that Cicero's view is correct, and Varro's view incorrect. He does not agree with the "conventional treatment of Cicero", which is not very favorable to this trivial philosopher. This treatment, says Voegelin, coming

[174]L.c., p. 86.
[175]L.c., p. 88.
[176]L.c., p. 89.
[177]Ibid.

to the assistance of the defender of the traditional religion, "is apt to overlook that in his [Cicero's] work something considerably more interesting is to be found," which – according to Voegelin is evidently important enough to make us revise our opinion of Cicero. This is "the archaic experience of social order before its dissolution through the experience of the mystic philosophers."[178] "The archaic experience of social order" is an obscuring phrase referring to the fact that in early times the social order was considered to be of divine origin. It is an "experience" which has by no means been dissolved but, on the contrary, confirmed by the "experience of the mystic philosophers," whose merit is according to Voegelin that they discovered the truth of God. What else is the archaic experience of social order but the belief that a society represents the truth of God, of course the truth of their own national God or gods. But this inconsistency is irrelevant in this connection. What counts is that the new science of politics confirms Cicero in his opposition to Varro: "Romans like Cicero understood the problem quite well."[179] Which problem? The question as to whether gods are the creation of society or society the creation of gods? And Cicero understood this problem quite well by advocating the second view?

The only point in which Cicero's philosophy does not get the unreserved approval of the new science of politics is his refusal to follow Greek philosophy in matters of religion. Voegelin explains this attitude as follows: "Rome was the Rome of its gods into every detail of daily routine; to participate experientially in the spiritual revolution of philosophy would have implied the recognition that the Rome of the ancestors was finished and that a new order was in the making into which the Romans would have to merge – as the Greeks had to merge, whether they liked it or not, into the imperial constructions of Alexander and the Diadochi and finally of Rome."[180] By "revolution of philosophy" Voegelin means in the first place the metaphysics of Plato and Aristotle. But both metaphysicians were most anxious not to make dubious by their speculations the authority of the established religion of the state. For Plato and Aristotle Athens was the Athens of its gods, just as for Cicero Rome was the Rome of its gods. To participate in this "revolution of philosophy" would certainly not have the consequence of recognizing that "the Rome of the ancestors was finished," that is to say, that the traditional religion of Rome could not be maintained. The metaphysics of Plato and Aristotle was quite compatible with this religion, as it was compatible with the – not very different – religion of Athens. There may be indeed a certain relationship between the transition of a city-state to a world empire and a

---

[178]Ibid.

[179]L.c., p. 90.

[180]L.c., p. 91.

change of religious ideology. But the non-participation in the "revolution of philosophy" could not prevent or retard such change.

In this connection Voegelin makes an interesting remark. When Rome merged into the empire, he says, and "the struggle between the various types of alternative truth, among philosophies, oriental cults, and Christianity" entered into a crucial phase, "the existential representative, the emperor, had to decide which transcendental truth he would represent now that the myth of Rome had lost its ordering force. For a Cicero such problems did not exist ... ."[181] But it seems that the problem of deciding which of the different "transcendental truths" proclaimed by the various religions of our time the modern state has to represent according to the teaching of the new science of politics, does not exist for this science either, which boasts of having discovered that society in general and the state in particular represents a transcendental truth, but does not bother with the question which of the many transcendental truths is the right one. Or is perhaps one of these transcendental truths as good as another for the new science of politics? This can hardly be the case, for, then, the new science of politics would be guilty of positivistic, and hence destructive, relativism.

The third problem Voegelin examines under the heading "The struggle for representation in the Roman empire" is the question how the republican city-state could develop into a monarchical world power. This is primarily a question of the change of form of government in its connection with the territorial extension of state power. It is only secondarily a question of the change of form of representation, insofar as the relationship between the organs of the state which are considered to be the representatives of the state and the mass of the subjects is constitutionally different in a republic from that in a monarchy. Voegelin formulates the problem as "the question how the institutions of republican Rome ... could be adapted in such a manner that an emperor would emerge from them as the existential representative of the Mediterranean *orbis terrarum*."[182] Voegelin's analysis contains nothing essential or new that could be considered as a contribution to the theory of representation. Its main purpose is to show that the glorious rise of republican Rome to a world power is due to the *Fuehrer*-principle. Following a recently published monograph, *Vom Werden und Wesen des Prinzipats*,[183] Voegelin points out that the principal institution which developed into the imperial office was that of the *princeps civis* or *princeps civitatis*, which he trans-

[181] Ibid.

[182] L.c., p. 92.

[183] Anton von Premerstein, *Vom Werden und Wesen des Prinzipats*, ed. Hans Volkmann ("Abhandlung der Bayrischen Akademie d. Wissenschaften, Phil.-hist. Abt., Neue Folge," Heft 15, Munich 1937).

lates: "the social and political leader."[184] "At the core of the institution was the patronate, a relationship created through the fact of various favors ... ", the relationship between the patron and his clients. "The emergence of the principate, thus, may be described as an evolution of the the patronate."[185] The result of this evolution is summarized as follows: "The patrocinial articulation of a group into leader and followers had expanded into the form of imperial representation."[186] Whether the doctrine that the principate had its origin in the institution of the patronate and, hence, whether the articulation was patrocinial, is here of no importance. Decisive is only that the new science of politics ascribes the emergence of Rome as a world power to the articulation into leader and followers. In view of this it is not superfluous to note that the phrase "articulation into leader and followers" is the literal translation of the German *Gliederung in Fuehrer und Gefolgschaft*, the fundamental concept of the political ideology of National Socialism culminating in the *Fuehrer-Prinzip*. That Rome on its way to a world power turned from a republic to a monarchy is a well known fact, what is new is only the description of this fact in terms of Nazi ideology.

It stands to reason that a monotheistic religion is a more appropriate ideology for a monarchical form of government than a polytheistic religion. Hence, the movement in imperial Rome toward the belief in a supreme God and, finally, the acceptance of Christianity as the most outspoken monotheistic religion, does not offer a particularly difficult problem. It is another topic dealt with in the chapter on representation in the Roman empire. Following, in this respect, the Dutch theologian Hendrik Berkhof[187], Voegelin ascribes the "surprising turn of events which in 311-13 gave freedom to Christianity"[188] to the fear that the powerful God of the Christians might take revenge by making trouble for the rulers if they prevented his worship. This may be true; but the God of the Christians would have not been considered as powerful if the number of his followers had not remarkably increased among the subjects of the empire, and if the Christian religion had not been recognized as an ideology useful to the government. To be sure, the attitude of the Christian movement in its beginnings was not very much in favor of the state in general and of the Roman empire in particular. The original teaching of Christ had certainly an anarchistic – and, in this sense, revolutionary – tendency. But it was against this tendency that St. Paul's spiritual efforts were directed, of which his letter to the Romans is the most striking symptom. In the fourth century A.D., St. Paul's doctrine that all state authority

[184]Voegelin, l.c., p. 92.
[185]L.c., p. 95.
[186]L.c., p. 97.
[187] Cf. Berkhof, l.c., pp. 41ff.
[188]Voegelin, l.c., p. 99.

originates in God was an accepted element of Christian religion; and such a religion could be used as an ideology of the Roman empire. Its incompatibility with polytheism proved to be irrelevant within a civilization characterized by an almost unlimited tolerance in the field of religion. Hence it is hardly possible to consider – as Voegelin does – the anti-polytheistic tendency of Christianity as a "revolutionary substance."[189] This revolutionary substance consists according to Voegelin in the fact that by rejecting polytheism Christianity de-divinized the world. "What made Christianity so dangerous was its uncompromising, radical de-divinization of the world."[190] Voegelin approves Celsus' critique of Christianity: "He understood the existential problem of polytheism; and he knew that the Christian de-divinization of the world spelled the end of a civilizational epoch ... "[191] But how is such revolutionary de-divinization, manifest already in the 2nd century, compatible with the fact, referred to by Voegelin, that the Christian theologian Eusebius, in the forth century, praised the emperor Constantine "because in his imperial he had imitated the divine monarchy"; and that this Christian theologian taught that "the one *basileus* on earth represents the one God, the one King in Heaven, the one Nomos and Logos," and saw in the *pax Romana* the fulfillment of eschatological prophecies?[192] That means that Eusebius recognized the Roman empire as a divine monarchy, the realization of God's will on earth, which is just the contrary of a de-divinization of the world. Voegelin thinks that the doctrine of the three divine personalities made it impossible to maintain the idea of the emperor representing the triune godhead. He refers to Gregory of Nazianzus' view that the Christians "do not believe in the monarchy of a single person in the godhead, for such a godhead would be a source of discord; Christians believe in the triunity – and this triunity of God has no analogue in creation." But Voegelin must admit that Gregory "declared the Christians to believe in the divine monarchy."[193] Hence the belief in the three divine personalities – not so different from a polytheistic religion – had not at all the effect of de-divining the world of the Roman empire, which, in spite of this belief, was recognized as a divine institution. Voegelin refers also to St. Augustine, who did not share Eusebius' recognition of the *pax Romana* as the fulfillment of eschatological prophecies of eternal peace, but, on the contrary pointed to the fact that within the Roman empire wars were going on. But Voegelin cannot ignore that Augustine did not exclude the possibility of the prophecy being fulfilled in the future; he quotes Augustine's statement; "but perhaps, we hope, 'it will be

[189] L.c., p. 100.
[190] L.c., p. 100.
[191] L.c., p. 101.
[192] L.c., p. 104.
[193] L.c., p. 105.

fulfilled'."[194] If this sentence is to be understood in connection with Augustine's re-interpretation of the Messianic idea, his doctrine that the *kingdom* of God will not be realized in this but in another world, this doctrine does not mean that the will of God cannot be realized in this world. For Augustine's teaching was not and could not be, in opposition to Jesus' prayer "Thy kingdom come; Thy will be done on earth as it is in heaven", which is not addressed to a God whose existence is restricted to another world. Augustine's theology, as any Christian theology, does not and cannot furnish evidence of an "uncompromising, radical de-divinization of the world" by Christianity. There is, especially, no reason for Voegelin's assumption that Augustine's counterposition "is the end of political theology in orthodox Christianity. The spiritual destiny of man in the Christian sense cannot be represented on earth by the power organization of a political society; It can be represented only by the church. The sphere of power is radically de-divinized; it has become temporal."[195] There was never a radical de-divinization of the sphere of power, for never St. Paul's teaching has been abandoned that "there is no governing authority except from God, and those that exist have been instituted by God."[196] It is just the divinization of governmental power which is a specific achievement of Paulinian Christianity. "The double representation of man in society through church and empire" – as Voegelin characterizes the dualistic organization of society during the Middle Ages – has nothing to do with a de-divinization of a society of which the church was an essential part and the empire a divine institution.

How impossible Voegelin's doctrine is that Christianity means de-divinization manifests itself in the fact that he is very ambiguous with respect to the object of this de-divinization. He speaks one time of a "de-divinization of the world",[197] another time of a "re-divinization of society"[198], and occasionally he restricts his doctrine to the assertion of a "de-divinization of the temporal sphere of power"[199]. But that this doctrine, even in this restricted version, is untenable, becomes evident in Voegelin's final definition. He says: "by de-divinization shall be meant the historical process in which the culture of polytheism dies from experiential atrophy, and human existence in society became reordered through the experience of man's destination, by the grace of the world-transcendent God, toward eternal life in beatific vision."[200] It can only be Christianity by which "human existence in society

[194]L.c., p. 106.
[195]L.c., p. 106.
[196]Roman, 13.
[197]Voegelin, l.c., p. 100.
[198]L.c., p. 106.
[199]L.c., p. 107.
[200]L.c., p. 107.

became reordered", and only human existence "in society" can be the object of this reordering. And if this reordering consisted in making man aware of his destination, by the grace of God, toward eternal life, then society was not de-divinized, but, on the contrary, radically divinized by Christianity. Voegelin's definition of de-divinization says the contrary of what the term to be defined says: the emancipation of man in society from the divine in general and from religion in particular. If there is such a thing as divinization of the world, it is the view that the world is created and governed by the almighty God and that consequently nothing can happen in nature or history without or against his will, that nature as well as society exists only through and with Him; which view is the essence of Christian religion in all its varieties. There is only one point in Voegelin's second definition of de-divinization that seems to justify it: the reference to the transcendence of God.

However, the transcendence of God has never been interpreted as incompatible with God's immanence. That the almighty and absolutely just creator and ruler of the world is at the same time transcendent to and immanent *in* the world, is one of the most essential elements of any kind of Christian metaphysics. To infer from God's transcendence that there is no God in the world amounts to a theology of atheism. And just as in Christian theology the transcendence of God is necessarily combined with its immanence, thus the immanence of God – which becomes most intensive in the mystic experience of the union with God, the so-called *unio-mystica* – was never interpreted in the speculations of the mystics as a negation of the transcendence of God. It is precisely the belief in a transcendent God which is the basis of the mystic experience, created by the passionate desire to bring God into the individual existence of man. That there is a logical contradiction between the transcendence and the immanence of God is, of course, no objection to irrational metaphysical, theological or mystic speculation. It is true that the existence of evil induced some theological speculation to the admission of a non-divine element in the world and to the construction of a kind of counter-God in the person of Satan or the Anti-Christ. But even the most radical dualism of a theological good-evil speculation could not lead to a de-divinization of the world. Just as the presence of God could not exclude the presence of the counter-God, the presence of the latter could not exclude the presence of the former. If there is such a thing as de-divinization, it is the tendency to interpret nature and society without referring to an unknown transcendental entity which, by definition, is inaccessible to human cognition. This is the essence of that anti-religious, anti-metaphysical science which Voegelin condemns as destructive positivism. If there is a characteristic by which so-called modernity can be distinguished from earlier periods of history, it is the development of this science which, with its tendency of emancipating the explanation of the world from religion, has de-divinized the world. In the introduction to his book, Voegelin says that for Max Weber "the evolution of mankind toward the rationality of positive science", postulated by Comte, was "a process of disenchantment (*Entzauberung*) and de-divinization (*Entgöttlichung*)."[201] Voegelin does not reject this definition, which indeed is the only possible one of this term. But, now, Voegelin uses it to designate just the opposite of an evolution toward rationality. For he embarks on the more than paradoxical enterprise to show that the nature of modernity is the re-divinization of a world allegedly de-divinized by Christianity. It seems that Voegelin has completely forgotten what he has said about the de-divinization of the world through Comte's positivistic philosophy. For among those who, according to Voegelin, are responsible for the re-divinization of society in modern times he mentions in the first place: Comte.[202]

2.3 Gnosticism a new category of political science

2.3.1 1.

In the history of religion by the term gnosticism a religious movement is understood which flourished during the 2nd and 3rd centuries, and was finally replaced by Manichaeism. Its characteristic feature is a strong tendency toward mysticism, which manifests itself by the conviction that the initiates possess a secret and strictly esoteric knowledge based on a mysterious revelation derived from Jesus himself. Gnosticism is one of the many mystic religions that came into existence at the end of -antiquity and, like all of them, it aims at individual salvation by means of certain rules, secret formulas, names and symbols, which have a more or less magic character. That gnosticism could be replaced by Manichaeism is due to the fact that both are fundamentally dualistic. Gnostic speculation, just as the religion of Mani, refers to the opposition between the two realms of good and evil, light and darkness, the spiritual and the material world.[203] It is in principle the same dualism as that of the spiritual and the temporal sphere, accepted in the doctrine of the medieval church, with the difference that in the gnostic-Manichaean speculation there was a strong tendency toward identifying the material sphere of human life so completely with the realm of evil, and of opposing it so radically to the spiritual as the only divine sphere, that the former could be considered somehow as de-divinized. If that movement is in question which in the history of religion is generally called gnosticism, its

[201] L.c., p. 22.
[202] L.c., p. 124.
[203] Cf. the article "Gnosticism" in the *Encyclopedia Britannica*, Vol. X. (1945), pp. 462ff.

aim is just the contrary to the one to which Voegelin attributes what he calls gnosticism. Historic gnosticism did not divinize but rather de-divinize – of course not the world or society, but – the material sphere of human life.

Although Voegelin devotes a great part of his study to the allegedly decisive influence of gnosticism on modern civilization, he is very vague concerning the meaning of this term as used by him. He gives nowhere a clear definition or precise characterization of that spiritual movement which he calls gnosticism. He does not refer to Corinthus, Carpocrates, Basilides, Valentinus, Bardesanes, Marcion, or any other leader of the gnostic sects, all belonging to the first centuries of the Christian era. He designates as "the first clear and comprehensive expression of the idea"[204], which he considers as the essential function of gnosticism, namely, the re-divinization of society, the work of Joachim of Flora, a monk and mystic theologian who lived during the second part of the 12th century (1145-1202), about a thousand years after historic gnosticism flourished. Voegelin does not offer any literal quotation of the work to which he attributes the decisive influence on the formation of modernity. He contends himself to give the titles of some recently published monographs dealing with this author and a general characterization of his main idea. What he reports as the main contribution of Joachim of Flora has nothing specifically gnostic in it, provided this term means what is usually understood by it in the history of philosophy and religion. Voegelin refers to Joachim's division of the history of mankind in three periods, corresponding to the three persons forming the one God according to the doctrine of Christian theology: an age of the Father, the leader of which is Abraham; an age of the Son, the leader of which is Christ; and a third age, the age of the future, which, Joachim predicted, will be inaugurated precisely in the year 1260 by a mysterious personality, the *Dux e Babylone*, a free invention of Joachim. The first age, although it was the age of the God Father himself, was the lowest in rank for it was only the age of the lay man; the second age is the age of the priest; but the third, the most perfect age will be the age of the monk. During this age of monachism the entire world will become a vast monastery and mankind will wholly be directed toward ecstasy, a feature that Voegelin does not mention. This is "the clear and comprehensive expression of the idea" which, born in the mind of an eccentric monk whose writings were condemned by the Church in the 13th century (1260, at the Council of Arles), has formed modernity, because it aims at a re-divinization of the world. "In his trinitarian eschatology", says Voegelin, "Joachim created the aggregate of symbols which govern the self-interpretation of modern political society to this day."[205] But why does Voegelin call Joachim's theology of

[204]Voegelin, l.c., p. 110.
[205]L.c., p. 111.

history "gnosticism"? The reader will find no direct and explicit answer to this question. He may only guess that it is implied in the following statement: "In order to lend validity and cognition to the idea of a final Third Realm, the course of history as an intelligible, meaningful whole must be assumed accessible to human knowledge, either through a direct revelation or through speculative gnosis."[206] Joachim's speculation is "gnosis" because Joachim conceives of the course of history as an intelligible, meaningful whole. Why the view that history has a meaning is possible only on the basis of "a direct revelation" or "speculative gnosis", is not understandable. This view has been advocated by extremely rationalistic, anti-metaphysical and anti-religious, positivist thinkers, who did not refer to revelation or gnosis; and were far from any attempt to divinize history, because they intended just the contrary, namely, to de-divinize history, Comte and Marx. And the opposite view: that history has no meaning at all, too, has been advocated in modern civilization. But Voegelin asserts: "Hence, the Gnostic prophet or, in the later stages of secularization, the Gnostic intellectual becomes an appurtenance of modern civilization. Joachim himself is the first instance of the species."[207]

Without making an attempt at showing that the Humanists and Encyclopedists were influenced by the work of Joachim, Voegelin simply affirms – what before him already Jacob Taubes in his *Abendländische Eschatologie* has affirmed[208] – that in their periodization of history into ancient, medieval and modern history, the three ages of Joachim are recognizable.[209] In another connection he says that the "conception of a modern age succeeding the Middle Ages is itself one of the symbols created by the Gnostic movement."[210] But when he starts his interpretation of modern age as gnostic revolution, and the Reformation, with which the modern age begins, as a "revolutionary eruption of the Gnostic movements", he declares that the problem when a modern period of history begins, "cannot be solved on the level of Gnostic symbolism."[211] That means that the gnostic symbol of history as a sequence of three ages and the humanist and encyclopedist periodization of history into ancient, medieval, and modern history have nothing else in common but the division of a whole into three parts, which is a general scheme of articulation or systematization, as old as human thinking. To recognize

---

[206]L.c., p. 112.

[207]Ibid.

[208]Jacob Taubes, *Abendländische Eschatologie*, Bern, 1947 (quoted by Voegelin, pp. 108, 111), p. 81: "The scheme: Antiquity – Middle Ages – Modern Times, is nothing else but a secularization of Joachim's prophecy of the three ages."

[209]Voegelin, l.c., p. 111.

[210]L.c., p. 133.

[211]L.c., p. 134.

Joachim's three ages in our periodization of history is as justified as to recognize the mystic trinity in the distinction between childhood, manhood, and old age. Our completely rationalized periodization of history can have nothing to do with Joachim's trinitarian speculation projected into history, not only because there is no provable connection between the two, but because their meaning is totally different. The three stages of Joachim represent an order of rank, the third stage being understood as a definite stage of perfection. Its purpose is evidently the glorification of monachism, and not at all a scientific analysis of history. Our periodization of history into three stages has never been understood as a definite articulation; only as a systematization from the point of view of our present knowledge of history, which may be replaced at any time and especially in the future on the basis of a more extensive and profounder knowledge. The concept of the third stage: modern times, is far from implying the idea of perfection and compatible with any value judgment whatsoever. It certainly does not convey the idea of a definite status of human civilization, not capable of further evolution.

As Dr. Faustus in Goethe's famous play, after having drunk the magic potion sees Helene in every woman, Voegelin sees Joachim's trinitarian eschatology whenever he finds a partition into three periods, in "Turgot's and Comte's theory of a sequence of theological, metaphysical, and scientific phases; in Hegel's dialectic of the three stages of freedom and self-reflective Spiritual fulfillment" and, above all, in "the Marxian dialectic of the three stages of primitive communism, class society, and final communism"[212] Joachim's age of the monk, he seriously contends, "has become a formidable component in the contemporary democratic creed, and it is the dynamic core in the Marxian mysticism of the realm of freedom and the withering away of the state."[213] It is not worth while to deal with the fantastic and in no way specified view that a prophecy made at the end of the 12th century to the effect that in 1260 an age of monachism under the leadership of a duke of Babylon – the product of the imagination of a mystic – has anything to do with the belief that democracy, that is, a government on which the governed subjects have direct or indirect influence, is a good government. But it is perhaps not quite superfluous to analyze Voegelin's – no less fantastic – interpretation of Marxism as gnosticism. For this interpretation plays a decisive part in the justification of his thesis that gnosticism is the very nature of modernity.

It is true that there exists a certain similarity – frequently pointed out[214] between the Marxian interpretation of history as sequence of a happy sta-

[212]L.c., pp. 111/2.

[213]L.c., p. 113.

[214]For instance, by Fritz Gerlich, *Kommunismus als Lehre vom tausendjärigem Reich*, 1920. Cf. also Taubes, l.c., p. 136.

tus of mankind during the period of primitive communism, followed by the unhappy period of society split into classes, and a stage of happiness in the communist society of the future, on the one hand, and a certain religious scheme on the other hand. But this religious scheme has nothing to do with gnosticism, nor with Joachim's trinity speculation. It is the messianic belief in the existence of a paradise at the beginning of time, which has been lost by the fall of man, but which will return with the kingdom of God predicted by the prophets. Although the similarity is *prima facie* striking, and although Marx might have been unconsciously influenced by messianic ideas, it is nevertheless not more than a surface analogy. First of all, because the correspondence between the paradise of the past and that of the future – essential for the messianic scheme – is of secondary importance in the Marxian construction. As a matter of fact, it is only Engels, not Marx himself, who is responsible for the doctrine that communism was the original stage of mankind and that this stage was one of perfect freedom, because a stateless and lawless anarchy. Engels accepted this doctrine probably only for the purpose of showing that a stateless and lawless communist society, predicted by the economic interpretation of society, was not a utopian imagination but has already existed in the history of mankind. The communist society of the future is not – as the kingdom of God is the return of the first paradise – the re-establishment of early communism; it is not a technically primitive, but a highly developed social organization. And, above all, the prediction of a state- and lawless communist society of the future is the result of a rationalistic, anti-metaphysical, critical analysis of social reality. In this respect Marx' philosophy of history is just the contrary of the messianic belief in a paradise, lost as a punishment inflicted by God and to be regained by the grace of God. It is an essential feature of revolutionary Marxism that the paradise of the future will be the work of man, in a world completely de-divinized by the most radical and most reckless critique of religion ever undertaken. There is nothing mystical in this social philosophy; and to speak of "Marxian mysticism", the supposed intention of which is a re-divinization of society, is to fly in the face of historical truth.[215]

By his visionary prediction of an imaginary duke of Babylon, Joachim – according to Voegelin's interpretation, has created the symbol of the leader, although the age of the monk of which this duke is supposed to be the "leader" represents the symbol "of the brotherhood of autonomous per-

[215]The situation is different with respect to Hegel's theology of history to which Marx expressly opposed his economic-materialistic interpretation. Taubes (l.c., pp. 90ff.) shows that there is indeed much more than a surface similarity between Joachim's trinitarian eschatology and Hegel's dialectic of history by referring to Hegel's view that the divine trinity is the essence of the history of the world.

sons,"[216] which is incompatible with leadership. Hence it is not too astonishing that Voegelin can discern the duke of Babylon, the leader of the age of the monk, in Machiavelli's *principe* and "in the supermen of Condorcet, Comte, and Marx."[217] The symbol of the leader is one of the oldest elements of social consciousness of man and did not have to wait for its creation by Joachim in the 12th century. If the nebulous duke of Babylon was imagined by Joachim as a leader at all, he was the leader in the sense of a patron saint of an age, the age of the monk, like Abraham was the patron saint of the age of the layman, and Jesus Christ the patron saint of the age of the priest. The patron saint of an age is something totally different from the *principe* of Machiavelli, the head of a small state. The "supermen" of Condorcet, Comte and especially Marx are visionary creations of Voegelin, no less fantastic than Joachim's *Dux e Babylone*.

Another symbol created by Joachim in the 12th century – though an essential element of the Jewish religion long before Jesus Christ – is, we learn from Voegelin, "that of the prophet."[218] It is "sometimes blending into" that of the leader. Hence it seems that Voegelin interprets the Joachitic vision of the three leaders to mean that these leaders are at the same time prophets. The personality of a prophet-leader is not an invention of Joachim. Long before him, and certainly well known by him, Mohammed entered the history of the world.

According to Voegelin, not only the most outstanding philosophers of modern times but also political movements, as e.g. National Socialism, can be understood only as manifestations of gnosticism or – what seems to Voegelin to be the same – as Joachitic mysticism. He says: "Hitler's millenial prophecy authentically derives from Joachitic speculation ... "[219] The idea of a realm of a thousand years has by no means its origin in Joachim's prophecy of an age of monachism; and even if it were possible to prove that Hitler, or those who furnished his political ideology, have taken over from Joachitic speculation the propaganda phrase of the *Dritte Reich* that will last a thousand years – which supposition Voegelin does not prove at all – "Hitler's millennial prophecy" has turned out to be a tragicomical joke, a political slogan that even the Nazi ideologists did not take seriously. But this is one of Voegelin's two examples of a modern political society whose self-interpretation is governed by the symbols created by Joachim's trinitarian eschatology. It seems, however, that Voegelin is not quite sure about Nazism as a gnostic-Joachitic movement. For later on he characterizes "the

[216]Voegelin, l.c., p. 112.
[217]Ibid.
[218]Ibid.
[219]L.c., p. 113.

Dritte Reich of the National Socialist movement" as a merely "nationalist, accidental touch ... due to the fact that the symbol of the *Dritte Reich* did not stem from the speculative effort of a philosopher of rank but rather from dubious literary transfers".[220] But just a few lines before we are taught that this symbol "authentically" derives from Joachitic speculation." Now we learn – what we already knew – that the "National Socialist propagandists picked it up from Moeller van den Bruck's tract of that Name." Moeller van den Bruck, who was not a Nazi, found the formula in the course of his work on a German edition of Dostoevski, who, as a fervent Russian nationalist, had accepted the ideology of Russian imperialism: that Russia was the successor of the Roman-Byzantine empire and as such the Third Rome.

This latter ideology is Voegelin's second example of a self-interpretation of a modern political society governed by the symbols created by Joachim's trinitarian eschatology. It is one of the arguments for his doctrine that gnosticism is the nature of modernity and that the re-divnization of the world is the essential function of gnosticism. "The third Rome", Voegelin asserts, "is characterized by the same blend of an eschatology of the spiritual realm with its realization by a political society as the National Socialist idea of the *Dritte Reich*."[221] But he says that the Third Rome is an "other branch of political re-divinization" and emphasizes that "Russia developed a type *sui generis* of re-presentation, in both the transcendental and the existential respects."[222] Nevertheless, he speaks of a "blending" of "later variants" of the Joachitic symbols "with the political apocalypse of the Third Rome"[223] and thus vaguely hints at some connection between the political ideology of Russian imperialism and Joachim's mystic theology. But the only document to which he refers as a source of the Moscovite formula of the Third Rome shows not the slightest symptom that could allow the conjecture that it has been influenced by the mystic speculation of the Italian monk. Voegelin's analysis of "the political apocalypse of the Third Rome" contains nothing that would make such a conjecture plausible. If, by the way, Moeller is the source of the slogan of the *Dritte Reich* and the source of Moeller is Dostoevski, then the Nazi ideology does not derive "authentically" from Joachim's speculation but from the Russian ideology of the Third Rome.

"After the fall of Constantinople to the Turks," says Voegelin "the idea of Moscow as the successor to the Orthodox empire gained ground in Russian clerical circles." Then he quotes a letter of a Russian theologian to Ivan the Great. The decisive passage runs as follows: "Know you, ... O pious

---

[220]Ibid.

[221]L.c., p. 114.

[222]L.c., p. 116.

[223]L.c., p. 117.

Tsar that all empires of the orthodox Christians have converged into thine own. You are the sole autocrat of the universe, the only tsar of all Christians ... According to the prophetic books all Christian empires have an end and will converge into one empire, that of our gossudar, that is, into the Empire of Russia. Two Romes have fallen, but the third will last, and there will not be a fourth one."[224] A submissive servant of an autocrat expresses in a way for which the term "Byzantinism" has been coined, the opinion that his master has the right to subjugate to his rule all other countries and that his rule will last forever. In order to justify the imperialistic policy of the "autocrat of the Universe," he furnishes a religious ideology; which is his professional function. There is nothing mystic in this manifestation of theologian servility. The idea of the Third Rome as the never ending rule of the Russian gossudars is based on "the prophetic books," which, if indicating a definite source, can mean only that part of the Holy Scripture which is called the Books of the Prophets, and on no gnostic or other mystic source whatsoever.

Voegelin's attempt to use the Russian Caesaro-papism as an argument for the political re-divinization of the world, as the essential meaning of modernity, is particularly unfortunate. For, in contradistinction to the doctrine prevailing in the West that the Pope as the head of the Church is, if not superior to, at least independent of the emperor as the head of the state, the Russian Caesaro-papism, "with its tendency toward transforming the church into a civil institution,"[225] means that the emperor as the head of the state, representing the temporal sphere, is at the same time the head of the church, representing the spiritual sphere; which is much nearer to a *de-* than to a *re-*divinization of society.

2.3.2 2.

The new science of politics does not restrict itself to the bold assertion that the Joachitic eschatology has positively affected modern politics and that Western political societies interpret the meaning of their existence through symbols produced by this eschatology; it undertakes also a "critical analysis of its principal aspects."[226] But what it criticizes is not the principal aspects of the specific form this eschatology has assumed in the speculation of Joachim of Floris – the prediction of an age of monachism – but simply Joachim's attempt to find a meaning or – as Voegelin prefers to say – an "eidos" in history. This attempt is not specific to the mystic theology of Joachim of Floris; it is essential to any theological interpretation of history.

[224] L.c., pp. 114f.
[225] L.c., p. 159.
[226] L.c., p. 118.

For if, as theology must presuppose, mankind is created by a God endowed with absolute reason, it must have been created for some purpose, and consequently its existence in time, governed by the all powerful and absolutely just God, must have some meaning. Joachim was certainly not the first who interpreted history in this way. His idea that history aims at a definite, perfect state of mankind is evidently modeled after the messianic scheme.

Karl Löwith, whose *Meaning in History*[227] is – besides Taubes' *Abendländische Eschatologie* – the main source of Voegelin's view of Joachim's trinitarian eschatology and its influence on modern philosophies of history, says that Joachim's "interpretation of the angel of the apocalypse (Rev. 7:2) as the *novus dux* entitled to 'renovate the Christian religion' " meant "that a messianic leader was to appear, 'whosoever it will be', bringing about a spiritual renovation for the sake of the Kingdom of Christ ... " But Voegelin maintains that "the problem of an eidos of history," that is, the question whether history has a meaning, did not occur "in orthodox Christianity"[228], it arose in Joachim's eschatology, which was "a speculation on the meaning of history. In order to determine its specific difference, it must be set off against the Christian philosophy of history that was traditional at the time, that is, against Augustinian speculation."[229] However, according to the traditional Christian philosophy of history prevailing in the 12th century history had a definite meaning. For Augustine, just as for Joachim, the meaning of history was salvation. In the chapter on Augustine's Theology of History Löwith says: "What really matters in history, according to Augustine, is not the transitory greatness of empires, but salvation or damnation in a world to come. His fixed viewpoint for the understanding of the present and past events is the final consummation in the future: last judgment and resurrection. This final goal is the counterpart of the first beginning of human history in creation and original sin."[230] "The whole of Augustine's work serves the purpose of vindicating God in history."[231] Long before Joachim, Augustine distinguished several epochs in history, not, as Joachim did, three periods according to the three personalities of God, but – more "historically" – six periods according to the six days of creation. "The first extends from Adam to the Great Flood, the second from Noah to Abraham, and the third from Abraham to David, with Nimrod and Nimus as their wicked counterparts. The fourth epoch extends from David to the Babylonian Exile, the fifth from there to the birth of Christ. The sixth and last epoch, finally, extends from the

[227]Karl Löwith, *Meaning in History*, 1949, p. 151.
[228]Voegelin, l.c., p. 119.
[229]L.c., p. 118.
[230]Löwith, l.c., p. 168.
[231]L.c., p. 170.

first to the second coming of Christ at the end of the world."[232] Orosius, the disciple of Augustine, too, recognized salvation as the meaning of history; guided by the conviction "that God governs the course of human history" and "all power derives ultimately from God", he distinguished four periods, represented by four kingdoms: first, the Babylonian, then the Macedonian, later the African, and finally the Roman kingdom. "This meaningful succession, culminating in Christian Rome, indicates that 'one God has directed the course of history in the beginning for the Babylonians, and in the end for the Romans."[233] In view of these facts it is hardly possible to maintain that the problem of an eidos in history did not occur in orthodox Christianity and that this problem first arose in Joachim's trinitarian eschatology, and, in particular, that it arose "from the Joachitic immanentization."[234]

By "immanentization" Voegelin means that whereas Augustine projected the fulfillment of the Christian expectation of the kingdom of God into another world, Joachim – in conformity with the original messianic idea of the kingdom of God – predicted its realization on earth, in the future of monachism. This tendency of Joachim's eschatology is characterized by Voegelin as follows: "The age of Joachim would bring an increase of fulfillment within history, but the increase would not be due to an immanent eruption; it would come through a new transcendental irruption of the spirit."[235] By the bombastic term "transcendental irruption of the spirit" – in contradistinction to "immanent eruption" – Voegelin evidently wants to express the re-divinization of the world. But neither the Messianic kingdom of God on earth nor Joachim's age of monachism mean that God, the divine spirit, will enter a world completely forsaken by God; just as Augustine's transfer of the kingdom of God into another world did not mean that this world is completely separated from God. Such an idea is incompatible with Christian religion. Hence "Joachitic immanentization" cannot be interpreted as re-divinization. Anyway, this immanentization is certainly not the only way to find a meaning in history. Voegelin's statement: "The problem of an eidos in history, hence, arises only when Christian transcendental fulfillment becomes immanentized"[236] is without foundation. But he is right when he emphasizes: "Such an immanentist hypostasis of the eschaton ... is a theoretical fallacy. Things are not things, nor do they have essences, by arbitrary declaration." And then he arrives at the highly rationalistic truth: "The course of history as a whole is no object of experience; history has no eidos, because the course of history extends into the unknown future. The meaning of his-

[232]L.c., pp. 170f.

[233]L.c., p. 176f.

[234]Voegelin, l.c., p. 119.

[235]Ibid.

[236]L.c., p. 120.

tory, thus, is an illusion."[237] This truth has been found, long before Voegelin undertook his crusade against the destructive positivism, by a representative of the positivistic science of history, Theodor Lessing, who, at the beginning of the 20th century, published a book under the title *Geschichte als Sinngebung des Sinnlosen* (History as Attribution of Meaning to the Meaningless).[238] In this book Lessing calls "the view that history reflects reason and meaning, progress and justice", a "pious delusion." He refutes the opinion "that history is to be written on the basis of a science attributing meaning to its object," that "historic reality is a chain of causes having meaningful effects, revealing in the course of events a natural or even divine reason."[239] Voegelin does not mention this predecessor in the discovery that history has no meaning. And this is quite understandable, for Theodor Lessing belongs to a school of historians which is far from theologico-metaphysical speculations. Less understandable is how Voegelin can try to make the followers of the new science of politics believe that his rationalistic sceptical view that we cannot find any meaning in history, that history has no meaning because it extends into the unknown future, is compatible with his anti-positivistic postulate that the new science of politics has to be based on metaphysical speculation and theological symbolization. For it is just metaphysics and theology that are guilty of the fallacious "illusion" of finding a meaning in history, because the fact that the future is unknown to men does not at all prevent them from speculating about the unknown in general and the unknown future in particular, whether it be the unknown future of all mankind or the unknown future of the individual man, his fate after death, the "truth of the soul" discovered by Plato and taught by Christian theology, and just for this reason highly praised by Voegelin. Is gnosticism or what Voegelin designates by this term not of the same flesh as Plato's metaphysics and Christian theology? And if there is a difference, it is because gnosticism is still more intensive in its drive toward the unknown transcendental sphere than Plato's metaphysics and Christian theology, to the principles of which according to Voegelin the science of politics has to return in order to become again constructive. If such a political science has anything to object against the positivists Comte and Marx, it cannot be that they tried to find a meaning in history and that the meaning they thought they had found is – in the opinion of Voegelin – somehow similar to that which a theological-metaphysical speculation like Joachim's trinitarian eschatology has discovered.

As for the rest, to find a meaning in history does not necessarily presuppose a metaphysical hypothesis, that is to say, the recourse to a transcen-

[237] Ibid.

[238] Theodor Lessing, Geschichte als Sinngebung des Sinnlosen, 3rd ed., Muenchen 1921.

[239] L.c., pp. 3f.

dental sphere. By the meaning of history nothing else may be understood but that the social life of men and its evolution, just as nature, is determined by laws; and to find out these socio-historical laws is to find out the meaning of history. Whether this view is correct or not, whether it is possible to find out laws of evolution in history, is another question. But just as natural science in its attempt at describing natural phenomena in accordance with laws or a law of evolution formulated on the basis of facts, an analogous interpretation of history is, in principle, possible without any metaphysical hypothesis. This was certainly the intention of Marx who predicted the communist society of the future as the outcome of a law of social evolution, just as an astronomer predicts an eclipse of the sun. The law he believed he had found might have been a product of his wishful thinking of his desire for the realization of socialism. That he presented the realization of socialism as the outcome of a law of evolution is due to the influence that the evolutionary, anti-theological natural science of his time had on his thinking, and certainly not to any mystic speculation.

After denouncing the gnostic belief in a meaning of history as a fallacious illusion, Voegelin tries to explain why men deceive themselves and others by such an illusion. The reason is not, he asserts, "that the thinkers who indulged in it were not intelligent enough to penetrate it. Or that they penetrated it but propagated it nevertheless for some obscure evil reason."[240] The true reason is: the feeling of uncertainty. By "their fallacious construction" the thinkers "achieved a certainty about the meaning of history, and about their own place in it, which otherwise they would not have had."[241] Then Voegelin asks: "What specific uncertainty was so disturbing that it had to be overcome" by the fallacious illusion of gnostic speculation about the meaning of history? His answer to this question is one of the most original paradoxes of a study so rich in paradoxical statements. The feeling of uncertainty that had to be overcome by the fallacious illusion of gnosticism is that feeling of uncertainty which is the result of Christian belief. "Uncertainty is the very essence of Christianity."[242] Until now we were of the opinion that the essence of Christianity is just the feeling of certainty which an all-powerful, absolutely just and at the same time all-merciful God, whose will is done in heaven as well as on earth, gives to the believer; and that nobody can be so firmly convinced that history has a meaning as a Christian who believes that an omniscient, infinitely wise spirit directs its course for the best of mankind. To give to his incredible statement about uncertainty as "essence of Christianity" some appearance of credibility Voegelin repeats

---

[240] Voegelin, l.c., p. 121.

[241] L.c., p. 122.

[242] Ibid.

his unfounded assertion that Christianity by its victory over paganism has de-divinized the world. "The feeling of security in a 'world full of gods is lost with the gods themselves; when the world is de-divinized, communication with the world-transcendent God is reduced to the tenuous bond of faith, in the sense of Heb.11:1 ... "[243] Faith, according to this letter of St. Paul, is "the assurance of things hoped for, the conviction of things not seen." Any belief in God is a conviction of things not seen. If this belief is by its very nature "tenuous" and, as Voegelin says, "may snap easily", there never has been a firm belief in God, which, of course, is in open contradiction to facts. The view that polytheism, with its inevitable consequence of human-like gods acting one against another, as e.g. Zeus and Hera, gives man a greater feeling of certainty than Christian monotheism, is refutable by the undeniable fact that the victory of Christianity over the religion of Rome is due to a great extent just to the feeling of absolute certainty the believers in Christ gained by this belief.

The meaning of history is according to Christianity as well as to gnosticism (or what Voegelin calls gnosticism) salvation in a coming realm; and the coming is in both cases absolutely certain. Hence the question where and when it will take place can make no difference with respect to the feeling of certainty of the individual believer. And, indeed, in order to explain how through the gnostic immanentization the certainty can be achieved which the traditional Christian religion cannot guarantee, Voegelin applies the term "immanentization" with a new meaning. Now it does mean a "fallacious construction", a wrong theory about the meaning of history, the "fallacious immanentization of the Christian eschaton,"[244] that is to say, the transfer of the realm to come from heaven to earth, a historical period. It designates a religious experience in the soul of the individual. Voegelin assumes, it seems, that in the 12th century "a fall from faith in the Christian sense ... as a mass phenomenon" occurred: for he maintains that those who lost their Christian faith fell into the gnostic movement of this time. "The fall could be caught only by experiential alternatives, sufficiently close to the experience of faith that only a discerning eye would see the difference, but receding far enough from it to remedy the uncertainty of faith in the strict sense. Such alternative experiences were at hand in the gnosis which had accompanied Christianity from its very beginnings."[245] The religious experience, very close to the experience of Christian faith but nevertheless different from it, is the "immanentization" through which that certainty is achieved which Christian faith cannot bring about. It is characterized as follows: "The attempt at imma-

[243] L.c., p. 122.
[244] L.c., p. 121.
[245] L.c., pp. 123, 124.

nentizing the meaning of existence is fundamentally an attempt at bringing our knowledge of transcendence into a firmer grip than the *cognitio fidei*, the cognition of faith, will afford; and Gnostic experiences offer this firmer grip in so far as they are an expansion of the soul to the point where God is drawn into the existence of man."[246] The "expansion of the soul to the point where God is drawn into the existence of man" is the *unio mystica*, the typical experience achieved by a mystic in a state of ecstasy, the feeling of being united with God. "... the men who fall into these experiences", says Voegelin "divinize themselves by substituting more massive modes of participation in divinity for faith in the Christian sense."[247] This is exactly the deification of man and the assimilation of the creature to the Creator, which is the essence of a mystic experience as described by one of the great mystics, Meister Eckehart (1260-1327), in his *Opus Tripartitum*. If the immanentization as described by Voegelin in the just-quoted statements is gnosticism, gnosticism is pure mysticism; and then it is not understandable how gnosticism can become a category of a social science. For the self-divinization of man through his union with God is a most individual experience which has no social implication. The mystic is a-social. For his union with God isolates him from others. Self-divinization is no basis of social cooperation with others as equals. It stands to reason that such an experience is possible only on the basis of a strong belief in the existence of a transcendent God, and that the transcendence of God - as pointed out – is not only perfectly compatible with the immanence of God in the experience of the mystic but is an indispensable condition of this experience. Only because the mystic believes in a transcendent God has he the desire to draw him into his individual existence. Besides, the mystic union with God is a very rare experience in the life of the mystic, and outside of this experience God exists for him only in his transcendence. All this is nothing new, but it must be mentioned because Voegelin seriously maintains that the mystic experience of immanentization, the "operation of getting his grip on God" along with its self-divinization of man, is "the core of the redivinization of society."[248] Among those who are responsible for this redivinization, who fall off through their doctrines, induce men to fall into these gnostic-mystic experiences, he mentions Hegel and Schelling, some "paraclectic sectarian leaders" whom he does not name, and, above all, Comte, Marx and Hitler. In view of the fact that the gnosticism of Hitler and the gnosticism of Marx are note quite the same, Voegelin is forced to concede: "The intellectual symbols developed by the various types of immanentists will frequently be in conflict with one another, and

---

[246]L.c., p. 124.
[247]Ibid.
[248]L.c., p. 124.

the various types of Gnostics will oppose one another."[249] But, gnostics they are, even the atheist Marx. How can Marxism be an attempt at drawing God into the existence of man, at getting a firmer grip on God than the Christian religion affords, if Marx, following Feuerbach, declares the belief in God the most harmful illusion of mankind and religion the opium of the people; how can an atheist be a mystic; how can he have that experience which presupposes the passionate belief in the existence of God and which, from the viewpoint of an atheist like Marx, is nothing but the hallucination of an hysteric? Very simple: By taking an inappropriate metaphor for the expression of reality. Of Feuerbach and Marx Voegelin says that they "interpreted the transcendent God as the projection of what is best in man into a hypostatic beyond; for them the great turning point of history, therefore, would come when man draws his projection back into himself, when he becomes conscious that he himself is God, when as a consequence man is transfigured into superman."[250] The interpretation of Feuerbach's critique of religion – followed by Marx – that man himself is God, obscures the essence of his teaching, namely, that there is no transcendent power above man, that it is not God who created man in his image, that it is man who has created in his image this imaginary entity. Man cannot himself be God because there is no God. Hence, neither Feuerbach nor Marx exalted man to a superman. On the contrary. Marx calls the emancipation of man from religion, as an ideology of the existing social order humiliating man, the "return of man to himself," the "reconquest" or "restoration of man." Identifying man with God as an interpretation of Feuerbach's and Marx' critical destruction of the belief in God is fundamentally wrong, because if man is supposed not to believe in the existence of God, he cannot become conscious that he himself is God. To interpret the rationalistic, outspoken anti-religious, anti-metaphysical philosophy of Feuerbach and Marx as mystic gnosticism, to speak of a "Marxian transfiguration" of man into God, and to say of the atheistic theory of Marx that it carries "to its extreme a less radical medieval experience which draws the spirit of God into man, while leaving God himself in his transcendence,"[251] is, to formulate it as politely as possible, a gross misinterpretation.

According to the teachings of Marx – as according to any rationalistic, non-religious political doctrine – the welfare of man can be achieved only through man's own work, performed in confidence on man's own capacities and not by the grace of a transcendental authority. It is the principle: help yourself and do not rely on the help of God. This is the principle that

[249] L.c., p. 125.
[250] Ibid.
[251] Ibid.

Voegelin interprets as the Marxian transfiguration, as Marx' attempt at drawing the spirit of God into man in a more radical way than medieval theology, which left God himself in his transcendence. And on the basis of this interpretation of atheism as the most intensive belief in God he recognizes "the essence of modernity as the growth of gnosticism"[252] during which "civilizational activity became a mystical work of self-salvation", the "miracle of self-salvation."[253] As an example of modern philosophy which aims at such mystic-miraculous self-salvation by drawing the spirit of God into man, Voegelin refers not only to Marxism but also to another atheistic enemy of religion, Friedrich Nietzsche. He "raised the question," says Voegelin, "why anyone should live in the embarrassing condition of a being in need of the love and grace of God. 'Love yourself through grace – was his solution – then you are no longer in need of your God, and you can act the whole drama of Fall and Redemption to its end in yourself'."[254] Nobody, with the exception of the founder of the new science of politics, can see in these words of Nietzsche anything else but the unambiguous expression of the most anti-religious, anti-metaphysical, and consequently anti-mystic-gnostic, attitude. It is true that Nietzsche, in contradistinction to Feuerbach and Marx, spoke of a superman. But Nietzsche's hero was not a superman because he was able to produce the mystic experience of a union with God; he was, not a God himself, but a man above the ordinary men precisely for the contrary reason: because he was able to separate himself from God, that is to say, to emancipate himself from the belief in God, because for him God did not exist, "God was dead", God was "murdered" by him. The emancipation from the belief in God may be poetically called a "murder of God." But it can certainly not – even not with a poetical license be called a "gnostic murder"[255], as Voegelin does in order to maintain his impossible attempt to interpret atheism as gnosticism. If we are asked to believe that the atheism of Marx and Nietzsche is gnosticism, then we should not be astonished to learn from the new science of politics that Comte – "the founder of positivism"[256], of the destructive positivism that we have to abandon because it does not "rely on the methods of metaphysical speculation and theological symbolization"[257] – is a gnostic too, that his rationalistic philosophy is gnosticism, and that means mysticism. How does Voegelin work out this re-interpretation of Comte? Very simple, again by taking a metaphor for the real thing. Comte's quite insignificant remark that the memory of "those who contribute to civilization

[252] L.c., p. 126.
[253] L.c., p. 129.
[254] Ibid.
[255] L.c., p. 131.
[256] L.c., p. 130.
[257] L.c., p. 6.

will be preserved, whereas those who do not will be forgotten, is interpreted by Voegelin to mean that Comte guaranteed, as "a premium on civilizational contributions," "immortality through preservation of the contributor and his dead in the memory of mankind" and "the reception of the meritorious contributor into the calendar of positivistic saints," whereas those "who would rather follow God than the new Augustus Comte" "would simply be committed to the hell of social oblivion."[258] Thus Voegelin finds in Comte's philosophy the metaphysical belief in immortality, the recognition of saints, and last but not least, the threat of hell: "Here is a gnostic paraclete setting himself up as the world-immanent Last Judgment of mankind, deciding on immortality or annihilation for every human being." A more arbitrary misinterpretation of Comte's rationalistic positivism is hardly possible. Voegelin continues: "The materialistic civilization of the West, to be sure, is still advancing; but on this rising plane of civilization the progressive symbolism of contributions, commemoration, and oblivion draws the contours of those 'holes of oblivion' into which the divine redeemers of the Gnostic empires drop their victims with a bullet in the neck. This end of progress was not contemplated in the halcyon days of Gnostic exuberance ... "[259] Does this mean that Comte's view that only those who contribute to civilization will not be forgotten, implies the idea that progress will come to an end? This was certainly not the idea of Comte. Or does it mean that the murders committed by totalitarian dictators have anything to do with Comte's harmless prediction? If it has not this meaning – as we hope out of respect for an American professor of political science – it has no meaning at all. If Marx and Nietzsche, Comte and Hitler are gnostics, then, of course, liberalism[260] as well as totalitarianism[261] are manifestations of gnostic mysticism. That the one restricts the competence of the state to a minimum whereas the other expands it to a maximum, is of minor importance as compared with the fact that both represent gnosticism. Only one thing essential to modern civilization is left of which we may hope that it cannot be subjected to this forcible re-interpretation: modern science, the advancement of which is due to everything else but to mystic speculation. But the new political science is not inclined to justify our hope. For we read on page 127 of Voegelin's book: "Finally, with the prodigious advancement of science since the seventeenth century, the new instrument of cognition would become, one is inclined to say inevitably, the symbolic vehicle of Gnostic truth." "Scientism," that is, the appreciation of science, the readiness to rely on science, is according to

[258]L.c., pp. 130, 131.
[259]L.c., pp. 130, 131.
[260]L.c., p. 130.
[261]L.c., p. 132.

Voegelin "one of the strongest Gnostic movements in Western society; and the immanentist pride in science is so strong that even the special sciences have each left a distinguishable sediment in the variants of salvation through physics, economics, sociology, biology, and psychology." By distorting appreciation of science into "immanentist pride" in science and reliance on science into mystic "salvation" through science, the re-interpretation of modern science as a "symbolic vehicle of Gnostic truth" is achieved.

2.3.3 3.

According to the new science of politics it is not only the nature of modernity which is to be interpreted as gnosticism; but also the Reformation, with which the modern age begins, is to be "understood as the successful invasion of Western institutions by Gnostic movements." How does the new science of politics justify this revolutionary re-interpretation of the Reformation? Voegelin declares: "The event is so vast in dimensions that no survey even of its general characteristics can be attempted in the present lecture." Consequently he restricts his task to an analysis of "Certain aspects of the Puritan impact on the English public order."[262] These aspects are the religious ideologies produced within the left wing of the Puritan movement for the purpose of legitimizing the English revolution of the 16th century. Voegelin admits that "Puritanism as a whole cannot be identified with its left wing"[263], but he justifies his selection of materials by the statement that he does not intend "to give a historical account of Puritanism," that he is concerned only "with the structure of Gnostic experiences and ideas"[264]; and this structure can be found in the material he has chosen. But even if he had demonstrated the gnostic character of the religious ideology of left wing Puritanism – which he did not – his amazing interpretation of the Reformation, of which the Puritan movement was only one of many components and not the most decisive one, as the revolutionary eruption of gnostic movements would remain completely unfounded. Voegelin's interpretation of Puritanism is not based on an analysis of the movement itself but on the famous description Hooker gave of this movement. From this description Voegelin gathers the fact that Puritans in their criticism of the existing social conditions insisted on having a "cause", that the term "cause" was of recent usage and that probably the Puritans had invented it.[265] To have a "cause" in order to start a movement is interpreted by Voegelin as a "formidable weapon of

[262] L.c., pp. 134, 135.
[263] L.c., p. 151.
[264] Ibid.
[265] L.c., p. 135.

the Gnostic revolutionaries" How does this having a cause manifest itself? "In order to advance his 'cause', the man who has it will, 'in the hearing of the multitude,' indulge in severe criticisms of social evils and in particular of the conduct of the upper classes. ... The next step will be the concentration of popular ill-will on the established government. This task can be psychologically performed by attributing all fault and corruption, as it exists in the world because of human frailty, to the action or inaction of the government. ... After such preparation, the time will be ripe for recommending a new form of government as the 'sovereign remedy of all evils'."[266] It is absolutely undiscoverable what there is gnostic in this having a cause and in advancing the cause in this way, which is the way of any political movement directed against the established government and especially of a revolutionary movement. It is not specifically Puritan, and not in the least mystic.

Another symptom of the gnostic character of the Puritan movement is that it "relies on the authority of a literary source", namely, the Holy Scripture, and that "the leaders will then have to fashion the very notions and conceits of men's minds in such a sort' that the followers will automatically associate scriptural passages and terms with their doctrine, however ill founded the association may be."[267] This is the attitude of every political movement the ideology of which is furnished by Christian theology, without any gnostic or any other mystic implication.

The "decisive step in consolidating a Gnostic attitude" is according to Voegelin described by Hooker when he accuses the Puritans of "the persuading of men credulous and over-capable of such pleasing errors, that it is the special illumination of the Holy Ghost, whereby they discern those things in the word, which others reading yet discern them not."[268] Again there is nothing gnostic in the attempt of a religious leader to make his followers believe that he is illuminated by a transcendent authority. The "special illumination of the Holy Ghost" on which Puritan interpreters of the Scripture tried to base their authority has nothing to do with the mystic experience of a union with God. Only if Voegelin could prove that such mystic experience played an essential role in the Puritan movement, would his interpretation of this movement as gnostic in the sense of mystic be justifiable. But such a proof is impossible for the simple reason that no social movement can have such a mystic character, because the mystic experience has – as pointed out – by its very nature an anti-social or at least an a-social character. A true mystic is far from being even interested in a criticism or a reform of society, which was the main concern of Puritanism. A revolutionary mystic is a

[266] L.c., pp. 135, 136.
[267] L.c., p. 136.
[268] Ibid.

contradiction in terms.

In order to show that the movement which he calls the "Puritan Revolution"[269] is a Gnostic revolution, Voegelin refers also to "two technical devices ... which to this day have remained the great instruments of Gnostic revolution."[270] The first device is a "Gnostic koran", and the Gnostic koran of the Puritan movement was Calvin's *Institutes*. Why does Voegelin invent the strange term of "Gnostic koran" in order to characterize Calvin's work? Because a "work of this type would serve the double purpose of a guide to the right reading of Scripture and of an authentic formulation of truth that would make recourse to earlier literature unnecessary. For the designation of this genus of Gnostic literature a technical term is needed; since the study of Gnostic phenomena is too recent to have developed one, the Arabic term *koran* will have to do for the present."[271] But the Arab term *Qur'an* means nothing but "recitation" and the Koran is the Holy Scripture of the Moslems, considered by them as the word of God communicated to the Prophet Mohammed through the intermediation of an angel. Hence the Koran is itself a Scripture and not a guide to the right reading of Scripture as Calvin's *Institutes*; and hence it is by no means appropriate to call this book a koran. Nor is there any reason to consider an interpretation of the Scripture which claims to be authentic as "gnostic." The fact that Calvin – according to Hooker – claimed to owe his divine knowledge "to none but only to God" is certainly not a sufficient basis for such an interpretation. To be the mouthpiece of God was the claim of Moses, Jesus and Mohammed. If this claim is the criterion of gnosticism, the three religions founded by these prophets are gnostic and, then, the term "gnosticism" means simply religion. But Voegelin does not maintain the direct inspiration by God as the criterion of gnosticism. For he considers also the French Encyclopedia as a gnostic koran: "In the eighteenth century, Diderot and D'Alembert claimed koranic function for the *Encyclopédie francaise* ... " Why? Did Diderot and D'Alembert claim to owe their knowledge directly to God? This is impossible because they were rationalists. But Voegelin says that they claimed "koranic function" for the *Encyclopédie francaise* because they considered the Encyclopédie "as the comprehensive presentation of all human knowledge worth preserving."[272] Did they pretend that every word written in this dictionary had the value of an eternal unchangeable truth? They expressly declared to present in the encyclopedia only *l'etat present des sciences et des arts*[273] (the present status

[269]L.c., p. 135.

[270]L.c., p. 138.

[271]L.c., p. 138f.

[272]L.c., p. 139.

[273]D'Alembert, *Discours preliminaire de l'Encyclopédie*. Publié par F. Picavet, Paris, 1929, p. 75.

of the sciences and arts), which implies that this status is not at all to be regarded as definitive. Even Voegelin can attribute to the encyclopedists only the opinion that "nobody would have to use any work antedating the *Encyclopédie*, and all future sciences would assume the form of supplements to the great collection of knowledge."[274] This statement can only refer to a passage in D'Alembert's *Discours preliminaire de l'Encyclopédie* which runs as follows: "De tout ce qui précède, il s'ensuit que dans l'ouvrage que nous annoncons, on a traité des sciences et des arts, de manière qu'on n'en suppose aucune connaissance préliminaire; qu'on y expose ce qu'il importe de savoir sur chaque matière, que les articles s'expliquent les uns par les autres, et que par consequent la difficulté de la nomenclature n'embarrasse nulle part."[275] That means nothing else but that the reader can understand the content of the various articles without looking for explanation in other books, since for every term used in one article, but not explained in it, there is an explanation to be found in another article. D'Alembert continues: "D'où nous inférons que cet ouvrage pourra, du moins un jour, tenir lieu de bibliothèque dans tous les genres à un homme du monde; et dans tout les genres, excepté le sien, à un savant de profession, qu'il développera les vrais principes des choses; qu'il en marquera les rapports; qu'il contribuera à la certitude et au progrès des connaissances humaines ... " If that could be interpreted to mean that "nobody would have to use any work antedating the *Encyclopédie*", it should be added that it is said only with respect to the *homme du monde*, the educated layman, that the *savant*, the professional scholar, is expressly excepted; and that the reference to the progress of knowledge evidently implies that the *Encyclopédie* does not pretend to be the end of this progress. D'Alembert's *Discours préliminaire de l'Encyclopédie* shows clearly that by the publication of this work everything was intended but imposing upon the world a "gnostic koran."

In order to ridicule the uncritical way in which Marxists ascribe an undisputed authority to the founders of scientific socialism, it is usual to say that the works of Marx and Engels are the "bible" of their followers. This, of course, is an exaggerating metaphor. Substituting for the bible the koran, and taking the metaphor for the expression of reality, Voegelin arrives at his last example of a gnostic koran: "the works of Karl Marx have become the koran of the faithful, supplemented by the patristic literature of Leninism-Stalinism."[276]

The second device of gnostic revolution is "putting a taboo on the in-

---

[274]Voegelin, l.c., p. 140.

[275]D'Alembert, l.c., p. 150.

[276]Voegelin, l.c., p. 140.

struments of critique".[277] This is a device used by any religious movement which pretends to be in possession of absolute truth. To be of another but the authentic opinion laid down by the established authority is a punishable crime. The concept of heresy, which plays such a fateful part in the history of the Christian Church, implies this idea. To punish heretics and thus prevent a critique of the authentic doctrine is not practiced only by "gnosticism". The example given by Voegelin to illustrate a Puritan taboo on critique is significant. Hooker was blamed in the anonymous *Christian Letter* of 1599 – a document of Puritan origin – for having used Aristotle against Holy Scripture.[278] Does Voegelin seriously assert that the church, the representative of the "Christian tradition" which he opposes to gnosticism,[279] does not use this same device, that this Church allowed or allows free critique of the Holy Scripture? Voegelin can not deny that the Reformation was directed against the established Church as a movement which, at least at its earlier stages, set forth among its aims a free interpretation of the Bible. How, then can he characterize the Reformation as a whole as a revolutionary eruption of gnostic movements if he at the same time declares the suppression of this freedom as a specific gnostic device? If the nature of modernity is gnosticism, and if gnosticism means the suppression of the freedom of critique, how can the undeniable fact be explained that a characteristic element of modern civilization is the political movement toward democracy, which implies the principle of free critique, and that it was just with the Puritans of the Left that democratic theories originated?[280] The new science of politics does not face this question, unless the following statement is taken for an answer: "However well the constitutional freedoms of speech and press may be protected, however well theoretical debate may flourish in small circles, and however well it may be carried on in the practically private publications of a handful of scholars, debate in the politically relevant public sphere will be in substance the game with loaded dice which it has become in contemporary progressive societies – to say nothing of the quality of debate in totalitarian empires. Theoretical debate can be protected by constitutional guarantees, but it can be established only by the willingness to use and accept theoretical argument."[281] Does this mean that there is no freedom of critique in the Western democracies? If so, the statement is simply not true. And if Voegelin does not, and can not, deny that there is no taboo put on the instrument of critique – how could, otherwise, Feuerbach's and Marx' critique of religion and other ideologies have been possible in this civilization – and if

[277] Ibid.

[278] L.c., p. 141.

[279] L.c., p. 137.

[280] Cf. A.D.Lindsay, *The Modern Democratic State*, 5th ed. 1951, p. 117.

[281] Voegelin, L.c., pp. 141f.

it cannot be denied that the democratic creed is not based on a gnostic koran, like Puritanism on Calvin's *Institutes*, then there is no answer to the question how within a civilization the nature of which is supposed to be gnosticism, important societies do not use the specific gnostic devices.

As a specifically gnostic element of the Puritan revolution Voegelin considers the fact that the Puritan revolutionaries interpreted the kind of society which they were fighting for as the realm to come and as an event that required their military cooperation. On the basis of the most disputable statement that "there is no passage in the New Testament from which advice for revolutionary political action could be extracted,"[282] Voegelin assumes that the Puritans falsely justified their revolutionary actions by referring to the Revelation of St. John and arrogated to themselves the function of the angel who "comes down from heaven and throws Satan into the bottomless pit ... " To document this view, he refers to a pamphlet, *A Glimpse of Sion's Glory*, published in 1641, attributed to a Puritan. But the passages quoted by Voegelin[283] contain nothing that could justify the interpretation of the document as a product of gnosticism. With respect to the relation between the revolutionaries and God, the only relation relevant to the interpretation of the Puritan revolution as gnostic, the pamphlet – according to the quotations of Voegelin – says that the omnipotent God will come to the aid of the Saints, that is, the Puritan revolutionaries. God "shall do these things, by that power, whereby he is able to subdue all things unto himself. Mountains shall be made plain, and he shall come skipping over mountains and over difficulties. Nothing shall hinder him." Voegelin who first emphasized as a specific gnostic element that "a Gnostic who will not leave the transfiguration of the world to the grace of God beyond history but will do the work of God himself, right here and now, in history,"[284] must now admit that "the author of the pamphlet knows that not ordinary human powers will establish the realm but that human efforts will be subsidiary to the action of God"; whereby he drops this "gnostic" element in his picture of the Puritan revolution. Now he is no longer interested in the gnostic character of the Puritan revolution but in the fact that the ideology of the English revolution shows certain similarities with the ideology of the Russian revolution: "in this God who comes skipping over the mountains we recognize the dialectics of history that comes skipping over thesis and antithesis, until it lands its believers in the plain of the Communist synthesis."[285] That there are certain similarities between the ideology of the Puritan and that of the Soviet revolution is

[282]L.c., p. 145.
[283]L.c., pp. 145ff.
[284]L.c., p. 147.
[285]Ibid.

true; and the results of Voegelin's comparison are indeed very interesting. But the ideologies of all revolutions exhibit these similarities. To recognize the God who came skipping over the mountains in the Marxian dialectics, is one of the metaphysical exaggerations which play a not very fortunate part in Voegelin's interpretation of social phenomena. But even if the Marxian dialectics were identical with the God of the Puritans and the Russian revolution only a repetition of the English revolution, although the former resulted in a liberal parliamentarianism whereas the latter in a totalitarian dictatorship, there would not be the slightest reason to speak of both as of gnostic revolutions and to designate the dictatorship of the proletariat as a concept of "later Gnostics."[286] How arbitrarily Voegelin uses the term "gnostic" becomes evident in his statements concerning "gnostic wars." He says: "The revolution of the Gnostics has for its aim the monopoly of existential representation. The Saints can foresee that the universalism of their claim will not be accepted without a struggle by the world of darkness but that it will produce an equally universal alliance of the world against them."[287] It is obvious that this applies only to the Russian, not to the English revolution, since only the former and not the latter – in spite of its apocalyptic ideology – has aimed at a world revolution, i.e. at the revolutionary establishment of a new social organization comprising the whole of mankind. The fundamental difference between the two revolutions is obscured by terming them both as gnostic. Only on the basis of the unjustified assumption that the Russian revolution is a "gnostic" revolution, that is to say on the basis of an unfounded terminology, can Voegelin speak of the split into two worlds as of "the Gnostic mysticism of the two worlds." But the two worlds of the Joachitic speculation, the alleged model of the Puritan and Russian revolutions, the existing and the coming world, are not at all bent on mutual destruction. The split into two worlds is the result of the Russian revolution but was not at all the result of the "gnostic" Puritan revolution. Voegelin says: "The two worlds which are supposed to follow each other chronologically will, thus, become in historical reality two universal armed camps engaged in a death struggle against each other."[288] How two worlds which follow each other in time can become two camps existing at the same time one beside the other is indeed a mystery; but that "two universal armed camps" are engaged in a struggle against each other is no mystery at all. Nevertheless, Voegelin continues: "From the Gnostic mysticism of the two worlds emerges the pattern of the universal wars that has come to dominate the twentieth century." But certainly not the "gnostic" revolution of the seventeenth century! Since

[286]L.c., p. 149.
[287]L.c., p. 151.
[288]Ibid.

both are gnostic, Voegelin, referring to both, says: "The universalism of the Gnostic revolutionary produces the universal alliance against him", and thus arrives at the "Gnostic wars" of our time: "The real danger of contemporary wars does not lie in the technologically determined global extend of the theater of war; their true fatality stems from their character as Gnostic wars, that is, of wars between worlds that are bent on mutual destruction."[289] The gnostic character of these wars consists in the fact that they take place between two worlds "that are bent on mutual destruction." But the two worlds of the mystic speculation – the world of Satan and the world of God – are not at all bent on mutual destruction. On the contrary, only the one will be replaced by the other, and the other will last eternally. This is the case of the gnostic wars. They have just as little to do with "gnosticism" as the "gnostic" revolutions and the "gnostic" nature of modern civilization.

If the Puritan religious ideology of the English revolution is considered to be an essential element of modern civilization, then Hobbe's highly rationalistic philosophy, which much more than Puritanism has influenced the thinking of modern man, cannot be ignored in an analysis of modern civilization. Hence Voegelin quite correctly considers it his duty to deal also with Hobbes' *Leviathan.* Although this work is one of the first and most remarkable attempts to establish, at a time when theological speculation and natural-law doctrine were still prevailing, a positivistic political theory, Voegelin tries to locate also Hobbes within his all-comprising category of gnosticism. He says that the theory "which Hobbes developed in the *Leviathan*, to be sure, purchased its impressive consistency at the price of a simplification which itself belongs in the class of Gnostic misdeeds"[290]; as if simplification were a specific gnostic misdeed. He further maintains that the essential intention of Hobbes was to establish "Christianity (understood as identical in substance with the law of nature) as an English *theologia civilis* in the Varronic sense."[291] By *theologia civilis* in the Varronic sense, Voegelin understands – as we may suppose on the basis of earlier statements[292] – a theology that is a doctrine about God imposed by the authority of the state upon the citizens. Since according to Hobbes' political doctrine all teaching should be placed under the control of the state, theology too, could be taught only with the permission and by the authorization of the government. But this extension of the competence of the state to matters of religion has nothing to do with gnosticism or any other kind of mysticism. It is the rationalistic attempt to use religion as an instrument of politics. Finally, Voegelin

[289]Ibid.

[290]L.c., p. 152.

[291]L.c., p. 155.

[292]L.c., pp. 81ff.

maintains that Hobbes' *Leviathan* was "an instance of the general class of Gnostic attempts at freezing history into an everlasting final realm on this earth"; it shows Hobbes "own Gnostic intentions."[293]

To confirm this interpretation, Voegelin refers to a passage in the XXXth chapter of *Leviathan*, which he reproduces as follows: "He, therefore, declared it the duty of the sovereign to repair the ignorance of the people by appropriate information. If that were done, there might be hope that his principles would 'make their constitution, excepting by external violence, everlasting'."[294] Since Voegelin quotes literally only a few words, it is not superfluous to quote the whole passage: "So, long time after men have begun to constitute commonwealths, imperfect, and apt to relapse into disorder, there may, Principles of Reason be found out, by industrious meditation, to make their constitution (excepting by external violence) everlasting. And such are those which I have in this discourse set fourth: Which, whether they come not into the sight of those that have Power to make use of them, or be neglected by them, or not, concerneth my particular interest, at this day very little." This passage must not be interpreted without taking into consideration some preceding statements. At the end of chapter XXVIII, Hobes emphasizes that the commonwealth is mortal, and says that he will speak in the following chapter of its "diseases." Chapter XXIX begins with the statement: "Though nothing can be immortal, which mortals make, yet, if men had the use of reason they pretend to, their Commonwealth might be secured, at least, from perishing by internal disease." If interpreted in the light of these statements, it is evident that Hobbes did not predict the inevitable, because God-sent coming of an everlasting realm – the essential content of "gnostic" eschatology. He only referred to the possibility of constituting a commonwealth which would not perish by internal disease. He did not exclude the possibility that such a commonwealth will never be established, and he expressly admitted that even if it would be established, it might perish by "external violence." Hence the term "everlasting" used in the passage quoted by Voegelin is evidently a typical hyperbole, a slightly exaggerated expression of the idea of an internally stabilized regime. And, last but not least: Hobbes did not refer to a final stage of mankind, even not to a worldwide commonwealth, but to commonwealths in the plural form. There is not a shadow of a similarity between the realistic picture of Hobbes' Leviathan and the utopian stage of perfection mankind will reach in the realm to come according to the messianic prophecy.

---

[293]L.c., pp. 160f.

[294]L.c., p. 160.

2.3.4 4.

In the last chapter of his work on the new science of politics Voegelin deals with "The End of Modernity." Since the nature of modernity is gnosticism, we may expect to learn how gnosticism, and hence modern civilization will come to an end, and perhaps also what kind of civilization will come next. And indeed, Voegelin identifies the end of modernity with "the end of the Gnostic dream" which, as he says, "is perhaps closer at hand than one ordinarily would assume."[295] What does he mean by the "Gnostic dream"? The idea of an everlasting state of perfection. Gnosticism, he says, destroys the oldest wisdom that "what comes into being will have an end," and that "the mystery of this stream of being is impenetrable." Gnosticism is a "counterexistential dream world."[296] As a consequence of "its disregard for the structure of reality," gnostic politics "is self-defeating," because this disregard "leads to continuous warfare."[297] This is a rather problematical statement, since continuous warfare may have many different causes and is a phenomenon by no means restricted to "gnostic" modernity. But this statement is not the most questionable present in Voegelin's theory of the end of modernity. The "self-defeating factor" is only one of the two dangers which are inherent in "gnosticism as a civil theology."[298] The other danger is "the destruction of the truth of the soul."[299] That gnosticism is, or can become, a civil theology, is something new. Until now, we learned only that gnosticism has the tendency to establish a civil theology. Because Hobbes intended to establish Christianity as the English civil theology, he was classified as a gnostic, in spite of the fact that this attempt was precisely directed against gnosticism, the gnostic revolution of the Puritans. But how can gnosticism itself become a civil theology or, what amounts to the same, a civil religion, a state religion? What is the content of the gnostic religion? As far as this question is concerned, the new science of politics, which refuses to give a clear definition of gnosticism – as also in many other respects – is not very clear. We can only conjecture that Voegelin, when speaking of gnosticism as a civil theology, has in mind the political doctrines of Marxian communism and Hitlerite Nazism, which he characterized as gnostic ideologies and to which, indeed, applies that characteristic of the gnostic search for a civil theology that Voegelin formulates as putting a taboo on the instrument of critique. On page 187 we read: "As far as our experience with totalitarian empires goes, their characteristic feature is the elimination of debate con-

---

[295]L.c., p. 173.
[296]L.c., p. 167.
[297]L.c., p. 173.
[298]L.c., p. 166.
[299]Ibid.

cerning the Gnostic truth which they themselves profess to represent. The National Socialists suppressed the debate of the race question, once they had come to power; the Soviet government prohibits the debate and development of Marxism. The Hobbesian principle that the validity of Scripture derives from governmental sanction and that its public teaching should be supervised by the sovereign is carried out by the Soviet government in the reduction of communism to the 'party line'." But what has gnosticism as civil theology to do with the destruction of the "truth of the open soul"?[300] The truth of the open soul is – so we have learned before – the truth that the soul is open to God, that the soul is "the region in which transcendence is experienced" and that the truth of the open soul "is inseparable" from the "truth about God."[301] And, further, we were informed by the new science of politics that gnosticism is an "attempt at immanentizing the meaning of existence," the mystic attempt of "an expansion of the soul to the point where God is drawn into the existence of man"[302], which is nothing contrary to, but rather a still more intensive attempt at opening the soul to God, the most radical recognition of the truth of the soul. But Voegelin, speaking of the end of modernity, says: "The immanentization of the Christian eschaton made it possible to endow society in its natural existence with a meaning which Christianity denied to it. And the totalitarianism of our time must be understood as journey's end of the Gnostic search for a civil theology."[303] By the "totalitarianism of our time he" he can only mean Hitlerite Nazism and Marxian communism. That these political systems are "journey's end of the Gnostic search for a civil theology" or – as he formulates it later – gnosticism as civil theology, results also from the statements that gnostic movements, in their origin and development from Joachim to the Puritans, closely connected with Christianity, "tended to abolish Christianity,"[304] that the destruction of this truth of the soul "is the cause of the bleak atrocity of totalitarian governments in their dealings with individual human beings,"[305] and that it is difficult to foresee "the probable reaction of a living Christian tradition against gnosticism in the Soviet empire."[306] Since the National Socialist empire has already disappeared, the end of the gnostic dream and thereby the end of modernity seems to coincide in the main with the end of the Soviet empire.

It would be a mistake to interpret the "gnostic dream" of totalitarianism to refer only to the political ideology of National Socialist Germany and the

---

[300] L.c., p. 163.
[301] L.c., p. 67.
[302] L.c., p. 124.
[303] L.c., p. 163.
[304] Ibid.
[305] L.c., p. 164.
[306] L.c., p. 165.

Soviet state. It refers also to political reality. Voegelin speaks of a "Gnostic dream world." He admits, it is true, that "the nonrecognition of reality" which in gnosticism "is a matter of principle" does not prevent the gnostic politicians from remaining aware "of the hazard of existence in spite of the fact that it is not admitted as a problem in the Gnostic dream world; nor does the dream impair civic responsibility or the readiness to fight valiantly in case of an emergency. The attitude toward reality remains energetic and active, but neither reality nor action in reality can be brought into focus; the vision is blurred by the Gnostic dream. The result is a very complex pneumopathological state of mind."[307] This may be true to a certain extent with respect to the Nazi regime, but there is no sufficient reason for the opinion that the vision of reality of the Soviet government is "blurred by the Gnostic dream," that is to say, by their political ideology. The leaders of this Gnostic empire are anything but dreamers and their state of mind is not at all pneumopathological, whatever that term may mean. But later we read: Whereas in "the sixteenth century the dream world and the real world were still held apart terminologically through the Christian symbolism of the two worlds," later, with "radical immanentization the dream world has blended into the real world terminologically."[308] This "identification of dream and reality as a matter of principle has practical results which may appear strange but can hardly be considered surprising." But, surprising indeed, they are: "The critical exploration of cause and effect in history is prohibited: and consequently the rational co-ordination of means and ends in politics is impossible. Gnostic societies and their leaders will recognize dangers to their existence when they develop, but such dangers will not be met by appropriate actions in the world of reality. They will rather be met by magic operations in the dream world, such as disapproval, moral condemnation, declarations of intention, resolutions, appeals to the opinion of mankind, branding of enemies as aggressors, outlawing of war, propaganda for world peace and world government, etc. The intellectual and moral corruption which expresses itself in the aggregate of such magic operations may pervade a society with the weird, ghostly atmosphere of a lunatic asylum, as we experience it in our time in the Western crisis."[309] It is hardly possible that Voegelin considers the imperialistic policy of the Nazi and the Soviet governments as magic operations in a dream world, performed by nothing but moral condemnation, declarations of intention, outlawing of war, propaganda for world government. It is evident that now the gnostic dream world to which the just-quoted statements refer is not the world of the totalitarian states the political ideology of which is the

[307]L.c., pp. 168, 169.
[308]L.c., p. 169.
[309]L.c., p. 170.

civic theology of an everlasting realm of perfection; it is the politics of the Western powers directed against the totalitarian states which he castigates as "the manifestations of Gnostic insanity in the practice of contemporary politics." Now it is not totalitarianism that Voegelin accuses of identifying dream and reality, of prohibiting critical exploration of cause and effect in history, establishing its political ideologies as civil theology, putting a taboo on the instrument of critique. Now he does not criticize gnosticism as a civil theology of the Soviet society but wants to expose "the dangers of gnosticism as a civil theology of Western society."[310] Can he, under his responsibility as a truth-loving scholar, maintain that there is anything in the political system of the Western democracies that can be compared with that system which he calls the civil theology of the totalitarian states? If the most radical contrasts, such as the contrast between the liberal-democratic regimes of the United States, Great Britain, France, on the one hand, and the totalitarian-autocratic regime of the Nazi and Soviet states, can be comprised in the concept of gnosticism, this concept is an empty shell, and the combination of the term "gnostic" with "politics," "revolution," "civilization," and the like does not add any meaning to the second part of the combination. Still more serious than this misuse of terminology is the tendency behind it: to obscure the difference between antagonistic regimes. Voegelin says that the "nonrecognition of reality" in the gnostic dream world has as a consequence that "types of action which in the real world would be considered as morally insane because of the real effects which they have will be considered moral in the dream world because they intended an entirely different effect. The gap between intended and real effect will be imputed not to the Gnostic immorality of ignoring the structure of reality but to the immorality of some other person or society that does not behave as it should behave according to the dream conception of cause and effect. The interpretation of moral insanity as morality, and of the virtues of *sophia* and *prudentia* as immorality, is a confusion difficult to unravel. And the task is not facilitated by the readiness of the dreamers to stigmatize the attempt at critical clarification as an immoral enterprise."[311] The reader might think that these statements refer to the gnostic dream world of the totalitarian states. But the following passage shows that Voegelin is speaking of the "liberals" of Western civilization: "As a matter of fact, practically every great political thinker who recognized the structure of reality, from Machiavelli to the present, has been branded as immoralist by Gnostic intellectuals – to say nothing of the parlor game, so much beloved among liberals, of panning Plato and Aristotle as

---

[310]L.c., p. 173.

[311]L.c., pp. 169f.

Fascists".[312] It is not by Nazi gnostics that Machiavelli – whose *principe* is according to Voegelin the gnostic symbol of the leader – is branded as immoral, and Plato as a Fascist; and it is not the Nazi or Soviet theory that Voegelin accuses of establishing a "continuous Gnostic barrage of vituperation against political science in the critical sense."[313] Does he seriously maintain that outside the totalitarian states there is a barrier against any kind of criticism in the field of political science and does his statement imply that in the Western democracies a "political science in the critical sense" - which he evidently identifies with an anti-positivistic and anti-relativistic school of thought – is not allowed to develop freely? Can he seriously deny that this science, of which his new science of politics is a significant product, is no less, and even more *en vogue* in Western society than its opponent, and that to stigmatize its opponents as destructive, is not a vituperation? By publishing his anti-gnostic book in a gnostic society of the West he makes ample use of the essential difference which exists between this society and the gnostic society of the East, which difference he tries to eclipse by calling both "gnostic". As a "manifestation of gnostic insanity in the practice of contemporary politics" of "Western society", Voegelin points to the attitude toward the National Socialist movement as to "the Gnostic chorus wailing its moral indignation at such barbarian and reactionary doings in a progressive world – without however raising a finger to repress the rising force by a minor political effort in proper time."[314] Has he forgotten that by the gnostic insanity of the Western societies the Nazi movement has been destroyed after a very short existence? "Gnostic politicians," he says with indignation, "have put the Soviet army on the Elbe, surrendered China to the Communists, at the same time demilitarized Germany and Japan, and in addition demobilized our own army."[315] That means that the new science of politics disapproves of the policy of the Roosevelt and Truman administrations, and thus shows that it is indeed a "political" science, not a science of politics. Voegelin considers the "evolution of mankind toward peace and world order" as "mysterious" and does not believe in "the possibility of establishing an international order in the abstract without relation to the structure of the field of existential forces."[316] He is against disarmament as based on the erroneous view that armies are "the cause of war and not the forces and constellations which build them and set them into motion"[317]. It would be easy to show that the democratic politicians and liberal intellectuals he tries

[312]L.c., p. 170.

[313]Ibid.

[314]L.c., pp. 171ff.

[315]L.c., p. 172.

[316]Ibid.

[317]Ibid.

to ridicule as gnostic dreamers do not believe in a predestined evolution of mankind, but try to bring about peace and world order, without having any illusion about the difficulties involved in such policy, because they are fully aware of the forces operating against it, that they suggest disarmament or reduction of armament not because they are so stupid to assume that armies are "the" cause of war, but because they know – what nobody can deny – that the existence of an army makes war possible and that the militaristic mentality which is inevitably connected with the maintenance of armies is an additional motive for a policy which uses war as its instrument. Voegelin cannot obscure the fact that he distorts the ideas of his political opponents by referring to them as "gnostics." This term, applied to the politics of Western society in general and to the Democratic Party of the United States and the liberal intellectuals in particular, is degraded to an invective. Its true meaning becomes evident when he deals with the thesis "that Western society is ripe to fall for communism."[318] This pessimistic opinion – as Voegelin certainly knows – has been pronounced by the great economist Joseph Schumpeter whose anti-communist attitude is beyond doubt.[319] Without referring to this author, Voegelin says of the opinion advocated by him that it "is an impertinent piece of Gnostic propaganda"[320], that means: communist propaganda. Now we understand what it really means when, on the basis of the new science of politics, the Roosevelt and Truman policy, the movement for peace, world order and disarmament are called gnostic. It means exactly the same as what is meant when on the lowest level of propaganda those who do not conform with one's own opinion are smeared as communists.

One of the main concerns of Voegelin's theory of modernity as gnosticism is to accuse not only the Soviet state but also the alleged civil theology of Western societies of having destroyed "the truth of the soul", and to condemn the policy of these democracies as "Gnostic insanity"[321]. Among the Western societies "the American and English democracies" represent, according to his own testimony, "the oldest, most firmly consolidated stratum of civilized tradition."[322] England and America are certainly the most prominent, the most representative among the Western societies; and if the Western societies are guilty of gnosticism, this accusation must be directed in the first place at these two democracies. As a matter of fact it has been directed expressly at least against the United States under the Roosevelt and Truman

[318]L.c., p. 176.

[319]C.f. Joseph A. Schumpeter, *Capitalism, Socialism and Democracy*, 1942, and the same author, paper: "The March into Socialism", American Economic Review, Vol. XL (No. 2), 1950, pp. 446ff.

[320]Voegelin, l.c., p. 176.

[321]L.c., p. 170.

[322]L.c., p. 170f.

administration. But, finally, Voegelin admits: "Of the major European political societies, however, England has proved herself most resistant against Gnostic totalitarianism; and the same must be said for the America that was founded by the very Puritans who aroused the fears of Hobbes."[323] In the catastrophic situation into which gnosticism with its destruction of the truth of the soul has driven modern civilization, he sees – at the end of his book – "a glimmer of hope, for the American and English democracies which most solidly in their institutions represent the truth of the soul are, at the same time, existentially the strongest powers."[324] This is the – quite contradictory – truth of gnosticism as to the nature of modernity. It is in the end Voegelin's gnostic dream.

---

[323]L.c., p. 187.
[324]L.c., p. 189.

Kapitel 3

Nachwort: Voegelins „Neue Wissenschaft" im Lichte von Kelsens Kritik

von Eckhart Arnold

3.1 Einleitung

Es gibt in der Geschichte der Wissenschaft Bücher, die ihren außergewöhnlichen Erfolg weniger der Originalität ihres Ansatzes, der Tiefe ihrer Gedanken oder der Bedeutsamkeit ihrer Aussagen verdanken als vielmehr der Tatsache, dass sie den Nerv des Zeitgeistes treffen, indem sie Ängsten oder Ressentiments Ausdruck verleihen, die gleichsam in der Luft liegen, und die nur noch nicht deutlich ausgesprochen worden sind. Ein solches Werk ist Eric Voegelins 1952 erstmals erschienene „Neue Wissenschaft der Politik".[1] Dieses Werk beansprucht eine Erklärung für das große Übel seiner Zeit, den Totalitarismus, zu liefern, und es möchte zugleich einen Ausweg aus der Miesere weisen. Die Erklärung für den Totalitarismus, die die „Neue Wissenschaft der Politik" dann bietet, ist jedoch denkbar simpel und läuft auf die wissenschaftliche Rationalisierung einer gerade in den 50er Jahren sehr populären Vorstellung hinaus: Der Totalitarismus ist eine Folge des Verlustes christlich-religiöser Bindungen und Werte in der modernen Zeit.[2] Voegelin zufolge führt der Verlust geordneter religiöser Bindungen nicht etwa, wie man meinen könnte, zum langsamen Absterben der Religion in der Neuzeit, sondern ganz im Gegenteil zum unkontrollierten Wuchern besonders

[1] Eric Voegelin: The New Science of Politics. An Introduction, Chicago/London 1987. (Zuerst erschienen: Chicago 1952). Deutsche Ausgabe: Eric Voegelin: Die Neue Wissenschaft der Politik. Eine Einführung, München 1959.

[2] Vgl. Hermann Lübbe: Säkularisierung. Geschichte eines ideenpolitischen Begriffs, München 1965, S. 108ff.

ausschweifender Religiositätsformen, die Voegelin summarisch als moderne „Gnosis“ bezeichnet. In den totalitären Ideologien sah Voegelin lediglich den extremsten Ausdruck der wiedererwachten „Gnosis“. Diese im Grunde sehr naive Erklärung versucht Voegelin mit einem großen Aufwand an Fachtermini und komplizierten Erläuterungen in der Rang der Wissenschaftlichkeit zu erheben, so dass der Leser, dem jene populäre Vorstellung plausibel vorkommt, den Eindruck gewinnen kann, in seinem religiösen Ressentiment von der höchsten Warte der Gelehrsamkeit aus bestätigt worden zu sein. Darin dürfte der Hauptgrund für den Modeerfolg liegen, den Voegelins Buch in den 50er Jahren in den USA – und Anfang der 60er Jahre in etwas geringerem Maße auch in Deutschland – genoss,[3] sowie für das Interesse, das Voegelins Werk auch heute noch bei manchen Lesern findet.

Eine ganz andere Frage ist es dann, ob ein solches Werk einer sorgfältigen Untersuchung Stand hält. Bereits zum Zeitpunkt ihres Erscheinens war Voegelins „Neue Wissenschaft der Politik“ in dieser Hinsicht äußerst umstritten. Während Befürworter Voegelin als einen „analyst of civilization“ mit geradezu prophetischen Gaben bewunderten[4] und in der Neuen Wissenschaft der Politik „the kind of book that may well constitute a landmark in political theory“[5] und einen „wesentlichen Beitrag zu den Grundproblemen der Politik und zur geistesgeschichtlichen Ortsbestimmung der Gegenwart“[6] sahen, fanden Kritiker dagegen Voegelins Buch als wissenschaftliches Werk gänzlich unakzeptabel: „The almost complete lack of systematic evidence to support the argument of the book would alone remove it from the field of science.“[7] Ein Rezensent betrachtet es sogar „as very dangerous in trend – indeed as being as reactionary as anything I have noted in America in my memory“.[8] Fast durchgängig wird Voegelin – selbst in vielen befühhrwortenden Rezensionen – für seinen verworrenen Stil und seine unklare Sprache getadelt: „„...it is written in an extrodinarily awkward, polysyllabic language only distantly related to the one normally used in written discourse in

---

[3]Zeugnis davon legt die Fülle der Rezensionen des Buches in beiden Ländern ab. Eine umfangreiche Sammlung von deutschen und englischsprachigen Rezensionen findet sich im Eric Voegelin Archiv in München.

[4]F.R. Buckley: The Dreamers, Review of The New Science of Politics by Eric Voegelin, in: The Freeman, Vol. 5, No. 14 (August 1955), pp. 621-622 (p. 621).

[5]Review by John H. Hallowell, in: Lousiana Law Review - Vol. XIII No. 3 (March 1953), pp. 525-530 (p. 525).

[6]Rezension von Joachim Ranke, in: Zeitschrift für Staatswissenschaft 111/1, S. 173-179 (S. 179).

[7]Review by William Anderson, in: The Journal of Politics, Official Organ of The Southern Political Science Association, Vol. 15, No. 4, pp. 563-568 (p. 563).

[8]Review by George Catlin, in: Political Studies, Vol. 11, No. 2 (June 1954), pp. 174-175 (p. 175).

English-speaking countries“.[9]

3.2 Kelsens Replik

3.2.1 Die wissenschaftliche Bedeutung von Kelens Replik

Trotz der Fülle von Rezensionen gab es bislang keine einzige Replik auf Voegelins „Neue Wissenschaft der Politik“, die sich en detail mit Voegelins Argumentation auseinandergesetzt hätte. Die Kritiker Voegelins betrachteten ihn zumeist nicht als ernstzunehmenden Wissenschaftler und ignorierten daher sein Werk. Im kleinen Kreis seiner Anhänger und Befürworter scheint Voegelin dagegen einen Status der Unangreifbarkeit zu genießen, der jede kritische Auseinandersetzung mit seinem Werk von vornherein verbietet.[10] Die dadurch entstandene Lücke schließt nun Hans Kelsens umfangreiche Replik „A New Science of Politics“. Kelsens Replik stellt ohne Zweifel die bislang gündlichste und tiefgehendste Auseinandersetzung mit Voegelins „Neuer Wissenschaft der Politik“ dar. Aber nicht nur das. Sie ist zugleich eine sehr sorgfältige Analyse und ein umfassender Kommentar zu Voegelins

[9] Robert A. Dahl: The Science of Politics: New and Old (Review of David Easton: The Political System: An inquiry into the State of Political Science, New York 1953 and Eric Voegelin: The New Science of Politics: An Introductory Essay, Chicago 1952), in: World Politics, Vol. 7, No. 3 (April 1955), pp. 480-489 (p. 484). - Vgl. auch William Anderson, a.a.0, S. 568.

[10] Dies zeigt sich an der agressiven Polemik, der selbst eine maßvolle und wohlmeinende Voegelin-Kritik ausgesetzt ist. Vgl. Thomas J. Farrell: The Key Question. A critique of professor Eugene Webbs recently published review essay on Michael Franz's work entitled “Eric Voegelin and the Politics of Spiritual Revolt: The Roots of Modern Ideology“, in: Voegelin Research News, Volume III, No.2, April 1997, auf: http://vax2.concordia.ca/˜vorenews/v-rnIII2.html - Maben W. Poirier: VOEGELIN- - A Voice of the Cold War Era ...? A COMMENT on a Eugene Webb review, in: Voegelin Research News, Volume III, No.5, October 1997, auf: http://vax2.concordia.ca/˜vorenews/V-RNIII5.HTML . – Auch die Voegelin-Debatte, die jüngst in der „Zeitschrift für Politik“ statt gefunden hat, ändert nichts an dem Befund, dass eine kritische Diskussion von Voegelins Werk bisher noch kaum existiert. Die dort erschienen Beiträge beschränken sich entweder auf überwiegend paraphrasierende Darstellungen (vgl. Robert Chr. van Ooyen: Totalitarismustheorie gegen Kelsen und Schmitt: Eric Voegelins „politische Religionen“ als Kritik an Rechtspositivismus und politischer Theologie, in: Zeitschrift für Politik, 2002, S. 56ff.) oder auf Untersuchungen über die Genese von Voegelins Gedanken (vgl. Barry Cooper: Constituent elements in the genesis of Voegelin's political science, in: Zeitschrift für Politik, 2001, S. 243ff. – vgl. Tilo Schabert: Die Werkstatt Eric Voegelins, in: Zeitschrift für Politik, 2002, S. 83ff.) oder ermangeln von vornherein jeder greifbaren argumentativen Substanz (vgl. Arno Baruzzi: Kritik der Moderne nach Voegelin und Heidegger. Thesen und Fragen, in: Zeitschrift für Politik, 2001, S. 257ff.). Auch die vom Eric Voegelin Archiv in München herausgegebene Reihe der „Occasional Papers“ befasst sich bisher zum größeren Teil mit der Sichtung und Bekanntmachung von Voegelins Werk, wovon es allerdings erfreuliche Ausnahmen gibt (z.B. Hermann Lübbe: Zustimmungsfähige Modernität. Gründe einer marginal verbliebenen Rezesption Eric Voegelins, München 2003).

„Neuer Wissenschaft der Politik", denn Kelsen beschränkt sich nicht darauf, Voegelins Argumentation zu überprüfen, sondern er unterzieht sich auch der Mühe, die zahlreichen Verweise Voegelins auf die Geistesgeschichte nachzuvollziehen. Dies ist nicht zuletzt deshalb von Bedeutung, weil viele der Quellen, auf die sich Voegelin beruft, selbst Fachleuten nicht immer geläufig sein dürften, wie z.B. die Schriften des Paulus Diaconus.

3.2.2 Der biographisch-zeitgeschichtliche Kontext

Bevor jedoch auf die inhaltlichen Aspekte von Kelsens Voegelin-Kritik eingegangen wird, sind zunächst einige Worte zu den zeitgeschichtlichen Hintergründen und den Entstehungsumständen von Kelsens Voegelin-Kritik zu verlieren. Denn nicht nur als wissenschaftliche Auseinandersetzung mit der „Neuen Wissenschaft der Politik" ist Kelsens Replik von Belang. Sie ist darüber hinaus auch von biographischem Interesse, da Hans Kelsen und Eric Voegelin einander persönlich bekannt waren. Voegelin hatte bei Hans Kelsen studiert und 1922 bei ihm promoviert. Und obwohl Hans Kelsen und Eric Voegelin jeweils wissenschaftlichen, weltanschaulichen und – mit Einschränkungen – auch politischen Lagern angehörten, wie sie verschiedener nicht sein konnten, so war doch beiden gemeinsam, dass sie vor dem Nationalsozialismus ins amerikanische Exil fliehen mussten.

Hans Kelsen verlor 1933 aufgrund des sogenannten „Gesetzes zur Wiederherstellung des Berufsbeamtentums", das dazu diente, Juden aus öffentlichen Ämtern zu entfernen, seine Professur in Köln. Nachdem er zunächst in Genf und dann in Prag weiter lehren konnte, sah er sich 1940 zur Emigration in die USA gezwungen. Dort lehrte er zunächst an der Harvard Law School und ab 1945 in Berkely.[11]

Eric Voegelin erging es nicht viel besser: Nach dem „Anschluss" Österreichs an das Nazi-Reich wurde er von der Gestapo gesucht, konnte sich aber zusammen mit seiner Frau Elisabeth mit knapper Not in die Schweiz flüchten. Wenig später emigrierte auch er in die USA, wo er bis zu seiner Rückkehr nach Deutschland an der Louisiana State University in Baton Rogue unterrichtete.[12] Im Denken beider spiegelt sich die kritische Auseinandersetzung mit dem Nationalsozialismus auf eine sehr unterschiedliche Weise wieder, ausgehend von einem ebenfalls sehr gegensätzlichen Wissenschaftsverständnis.

Als Positivist hielt Hans Kelsen am Ziel einer streng rationalen Wissenschaft fest, die den Idealen der Wertfreiheit und der Methodenreinheit

---

[11] Vgl. Achim Bischof: Zur Biographie von Hans Kelsen, auf: www.hans-kelsen.de, S. 11-16.

[12] Zur Biographie Eric Voegelins vgl. Michael Henkel: Eric Voegelin zur Einführung, Hamburg 1998, S. 13-35.

verpflichtet ist und sich strikt innerhalb der Grenzen dessen hält, was der menschlichen Vernunft zugänglich ist. Seine agnostische Einstellung, die sich auch in der Replik auf Voegelin deutlich zeigt, hat Kelsen nie verhehlt, wobei er jedoch stets für die sorgfältige Trennung von Wissenschaft und Weltanschauung eintrat.

Im politischen Bereich bezog Kelsen eine liberaldemokratische Position. Bekanntlich war er einer der Architekten der demokratischen Verfassung Österreichs von 1920, und er verteidigte die Demokratie noch sehr entschieden als sich die Wende zum autoritären Dollfuss-Regime bereits abzeichnete.[13] Entsprechend seiner liberaldemokratischen Grundüberzeugung fällt auch Kelsens Staatsauffassung denkbar nüchtern aus: Der Staat ist für Kelsen lediglich eine Organisation, fesgelegt durch bestimmte rechtliche Normen, mit anderen Aufgaben aber nicht seinem Wesen nach von anderen Organisationen verschieden. Vor allem ist der Staat nicht Ausdruck irgendeiner vermeintlichen Wesenssubstanz des Staates jenseits der Rechtsordnung[14] wie etwa der Homogenität des Volkskörpers oder eines historischen Telos' oder – was in Richtung von Voegelins politischem Denken ginge – einer inneren seelischen Verbindung der Staatsbürger untereinander.[15]

Ganz anders dagegen Eric Voegelin: Voegelin kann bis zu einem gewissen Grade jener Generation auftrumpfender rechtsintellektueller Jungakademiker zugerechnet werden, die einem in den zwanziger und dreißiger Jahren um sich greifenden, lebensphilosophisch inspirierten Irrationalismus huldigten.[16] Die Angehörigen dieser Strömung verwarfen rundheraus die Wert- und Weltanschauungsfreiheit der Wissenschaft. Nicht mehr oder nicht mehr nur die besseren Argumente sollten zählen, sondern auch und vor allem die Tiefe des Erschauens und Empfindens, die Emphase des Gefühls.[17] Voegelin hat sich von dieser frühen Prägung später nie ganz lösen können. Der

[13]Vgl. Hans Kelsen: Vom Wesen und Wert der Demokratie, 2.Neudruck der 2.Auflage (Tübingen 1929), Aalen, Scientia-Verlag 1981.

[14]Vgl. Hans Kelsen: Allgemeine Staatslehere, Springer Verlag, Berlin 1925, S. 16ff.

[15]Vgl. Hans Kelsen: Reine Rechtslehre, Wien 1992 (Nachdruck der zweiten Auflage von1960), S. 290-291.

[16]Als Beispiel dafür, wie sehr Voegelin dem zeittypischen Jargon verpflichtet war, eine Kostprobe aus einer frühen Rede über Max Weber: „Im Tiefpunkt der Zerrütung, der auch die Sprache verfallen war, beginnt die allmähliche Neugewinnung des Bildungsgutes in Philosophie und Geschichte und ersteht der Schöpfer der neuen Sprache in Stefan George. Das Wunder der wiederholten Erneuerung wird viel beredet, und die Besten glauben an die ewige Jugend unseres Volkes als sein auszeichnendes Glück vor anderen Völkern..." (Eric Voegelin: Die Größe Max Webers (hrsg. v. Peter J. Opitz), München, FinkVerlag, 1995, S. 32.) - Vgl. auch die Einwände, die Leopold von Wiese anläßlich dieser und ähnlicher Phrasen in einem Brief an Voegelin äußert, ebd., S. 49.

[17]Vgl. Kurt Sontheimer: Antidemokratisches Denken in der Weimarer Republik, dtv Wissenschaft, München 1983, S. 54ff.

Vorwurf weltanschaulicher Verfehlung bleibt auch beim späteren Voegelin immer der entscheidenste Kritikpunkt, den er gegen von ihm abgelehnte wissenschaftliche Theorien vorbringt. Der irrationalistische Kern von Voegelins Wissenschaftsauffassung zeigt sich besonders deutlich in Voegelins Überzeugung, dass eine politische Wissenschaft im Sinne einer umfassenden, auch normativ zu verstehenden Ordnungswissenschaft ohne Bezugnahme auf Transzendenzerfahrungen des Menschen nicht möglich sei. Voegelin glaubte nämlich, dass es eine transzendente Seinsphäre gibt, die wir Menschen nicht mit unseren Sinnen wahrnehmen können, die uns aber in unserem inneren Empfinden mystisch erfahrbar wird. Ein derartiger Glaube findet sich in unterschiedlichen Spielarten in den meisten Religionen wieder. Voegelin weigerte sich jedoch die Anerkennung transzendenten Seins als eine Glaubensfrage zu betrachten. Vielmehr behandelt er die Existenz transzendenten Seins wie eine wissenschaftliche Wahrheit, und wer sie nicht glaubt, der hat konsequenterweise weder in der Wissenschaft noch bei der Gestaltung der politischen Ordnung ein Wort mitzureden.[18]

Komplizierter als Voegelins Wissenschaftsverständnis ist sein politischer Standpunkt zu beurteilen. In den dreißiger Jahren befürwortete Voegelin den österreichischen Kleriko-Faschismus, wie er im Dollfuß-Schuschnigg-Regime seinen Ausdruck fand. Dass seine Zustimmung zum autoritären Staat genuinen Überzeugungen und nicht, wie Voegelin es später in seiner Autobiographie darstellte, pragmatischen Einsichten entsprang,[19] zeigt sich sehr deutlich in seinem Werk „Der autoritäre Staat", worin die Frontstellung gegen das liberale Staatsdenken Hans Kelsens sehr viel ausgeprägter ist als die gegen nationalsozialistische Rechtswissenschaftler wie E. R. Huber und Carl Schmitt.[20] Nachdem Voegelin nach Amerika fliehen musste, scheint er sich jedoch nach und nach mit der demokratischen Herrschaftsform angefreundet zu haben, wenn er der amerikanischen Demokratie auch eine historisch-metaphysische Begründung unterschob,[21] die denkbar weit

---

[18] Vgl. dazu Eric Voegelin: Die geistige und politische Zukunft der westlichen Welt (Vortrag vom 9. Juni 1959), München 1996, S. 33f.

[19] Vgl. EricVoegelin: Autobiographical Reflections (ed. by Ellis Sandoz), Louisiana State University Press, Baton Rouge and London 1996, S. 41.

[20] Vgl. Eric Voegelin: Der autoritäre Staat. Ein Versuch über das österreichische Staatsproblem, Springer, Wien / NewYork 1997 (zuerst1936), S. 10-14, S. 24-34, S. 102ff. - Sowohl E.R. Huber als auch Carl Schmitt hatten sich zu der Zeit, als Voegelin den „autoritären Staat" verfasste, den nationalsozialistischen Standpunkt voll und ganz zu eigen gemacht.

[21] Vgl. Eric Voegelin: Anamnesis. Zur Theorie der Geschichte und Politik, München 1966, S. 353f. - Zur Kritik dieser Begründung, die sich auf eine sehr eigentümliche Deutung der für die amerikanische Verfassungsgeschichte in Wirklichkeit unmaßgeblichen „Common Sense Philosophy" des schottischen Philosophen Thomas Reid stützt, vgl. Eckhart Arnold: Die Bewusstseinsphilosophie Eric Voegelins (als Grundlage politischer Ordnung), Magisterarbeit Universität Bonn 2000, S. 118f., im Internet unter:

von der üblichen Theorie der liberaldemokratischen Demokratie, wie man sie etwa in den „Federalist Papers" niedergelegt findet, entfernt ist.

Die Beantwortung der Frage, wie Voegelin zur Demokratie stand, wird nicht zuletzt dadurch erschwert, dass Voegelin dem Problem der besten Staatsform höchstens eine sehr untergeordnete Bedeutung beimaß. Für Voegelin spielen weniger die Verfassung und die politischen Institutionen, über die ein Staat verfügt, eine Rolle als vielmehr die religiös-weltanschaulichen Grundlagen, auf denen die politsche Ordnung beruht. Sehr im Gegensatz zu seinen vermeintlichen Vorbildern Platon und Aristoteles, die die Frage der besten Staatsform ausführlichst erörterten, richtet sich Voegelins Interesse beinahe ausschließlich darauf, welche Transzendenzerfahrungen einer politischen Ordnung oder einer politischen Theorie (vermeintlich) zu Grunde liegen. Liegen einer politischen Ordnung echte und unverfälschte Transzendenzerfahrungen zu Grunde, so ist die politische Ordnung gut, andernfalls ist sie schlecht. Über die Maßstäbe, nach denen Voegelin die Echtheit von Transzendenzerfahrungen beurteilt, kann man leider bestenfalls sagen, dass sie höchst subjektiv sind. Trotz eines durchaus autoritären Zuges, der sich bei Voegelin mit diesen Überzeugungen verbindet, ist Voegelins ablehnende Haltung gegenüber der Theorie der Demokratie daher oftmals eher den aus seiner irrationalistischen Wissenschaftsauffassung fließenden Ressentiments als seinen politischen Überzeugungen zuzuschreiben.[22]

3.2.3 Die Entstehung von Kelsens Replik

Wann genau Hans Kelsens Replik entstanden ist, lässt sich – mangels einer Datierung des Manuskripts – nur ungefähr bestimmen. Da Hans Kelsen in einem Brief vom 27. Februar 1954[23] an Eric Voegelin mitteilt, dass er der Auseinandersetzung mit Voegelins Buch viele Wochen gewidmet hat (was angesichts der Detailliertheit von Kelsens Replik keinesfalls übertrieben erscheint), muss das Manuskript spätestens Anfang 1954, also nicht allzu lange nach dem Erscheinen von Voegelins „Neuer Wissenschaft der Politik" im Jahre 1952, entstanden sein.

---

http://www.eckhartarnold.de/papers/voegelin/node40.html .

[22]Wenn Voegelin beispielsweise im Aristoteles-Band von „Order and History" gegen Aristoteles Erläuterungen der Vorzüge der demokratischen Staatsform polemisiert (Vgl. Eric Voegelin: Ordnung und Geschichte. Band 7. Aristoteles, Fink Verlag, München 2001 (zuerst Baton Rogue 1957), S. 93.) so dürfte seine Abneigung wohl in erster Linie der durchweg rationalen und pragmatischen Argumentationsweise im III. Buch von Aristoteles „Politik" gelten und nicht so sehr der vermeintlichen Rechtfertigung der Demokratie, an der Aristoteles, der durchaus kein Demokrat war, ohnehin nicht viel hätte gelegen sein können.

[23]Der (kurze) Briefwechsel, der sich zu dieser Zeit zwischen Eric Voegelin und Hans Kelsen entspannt hat, und auf den hier und im Folgenden Bezug genommen wird, liegt im Hans Kelsen-Institut in Wien. Eine Kopie findet sich auch im Eric Voegelin Archiv in München.

Wichtiger als der Zeitpunkt der Entstehung erscheint die Frage, warum Hans Kelsen seine Replik nicht veröffentlicht hat. Diese Tatsache ist um so verwunderlicher als das Manuskript offenbar kurz vor seiner Fertigstellung stand: Inhaltlich erscheint es weitgehend abgeschlossen, und es weist, nachdem es mindestens einmal gründlich überarbeitet worden ist, kaum noch Flüchtigkeitsfehler auf. Der Hauptgrund für die Nicht-Veröffentlichung des Manuskriptes dürfte darin liegen, dass Hans Kelsen, kurz nachdem er das Manuskript an Voegelin geschickt hatte, den Plan zu einer umfassenderen Auseinandersetzung mit neometaphysischen Lehren fasste, in deren Rahmen seine Voegelin-Kritik aufgegangen wäre. Aber auch dieses Werk, an dem Kelsen noch mehrere Jahre gearbeitet hatte, und das unterdem Titel „Religion without God" hätte erscheinen sollen, blieb schließlich unveröffentlicht. Als Grund für die Nichtveröffentlichung dieses Werkes wiederum gibt R.A. Métall in seiner Kelsen-Biographie an, dass Hans Kelsen später zu der Auffassung gelangt ist, dass er seinem Werk einen zu engen Religionsbegriff zu Grunde gelegt hatte, der nur Religionen umfasst, die auf dem Glauben an Gott (oder an mehrere Götter) beruhen, womit sekularreligiöse Bewegungen nicht erfasst werden.[24] Dieser zu enge Religionsbegriff und die daraus resultierende allzu vereinfachte Entgegensetzung von religiös-metaphysischem Weltbild einerseits und rationaler Philosphie andererseits macht sich auch in Kelsens Voegelin-Rezension bemerkbar. Die Argumentation von Kelsens Voegelin-Rezension bleibt in allen wesentlichen Punkten davon jedoch unbeeinträchtigt. Leider bricht der Briefwechsel zwischen Kelsen und Voegelin ab, bevor Voegelin das Manuskript von Kelsen gelesen hat, so dass eine Erwiederung Voegelins, zu der Kelsen ihm vor der Veröffentlichung des Manuskriptes Gelegenheit geben wollte, nicht mehr vorhanden ist.

In den von Ellis Sandoz herausgegebenen „Autobiographical Reflections" hat Voegelin später die Tatsache, dass Kelsen das Manuskript nicht veröffentlicht hat, darauf zurückgeführt, dass er ihn zunächst vorsichtig in einem Brief und danach über gemeinsame Bekannte noch einmal deutlicher gewarnt habe, dass Kelsen bei einer Veröffentlichung durch seine Unkenntnis der klassischen Philosophie eher sich selbst als ihn, Voegelin, der Lächerlichkeit preisgeben würde.[25] Ob Voegelin mit der „brieflichen Warnung" auf

---

[24] Vgl. Rudolf Aladár Métall: Hans Kelsen. Leben und Werk, Wien 1969, S. 91. - Vgl. auch das Geleitwort von Günther Winkler in: Eric Voegelin: Der autoritäre Staat, a.a.O., S. XXV. (S. V-XXXII.). Winklers Version, die sich vermutlich auf Voegelins Autobiographie stützt, und der zugolge Hans Kelsen sein Werk unveröffentlicht gelassen hätte, weil er eingesehen hätte, dass er als Positivist bei geisteswissenschaftlichen Themen nicht mitreden könne, ist abgesehen von dem offensichtlichen Ressentiment, das daraus spricht, auch deshalb unglaubwürdig, weil Hans Kelsen ja auch später noch des öfteren zu philosophischen und geisteswissenschaftlichen Themen publiziert hat.

[25] Vgl. Eric Voegelin: Autobiographical Reflections (ed. by Ellis Sandoz), Louisiana State University Press, Baton Rouge and London 1996, S. 53.

seine Kritik anspielt, die er in einem an Hans Kelsen gerichteten Schreiben vom 7. März 1954 gegen Kelsens Abhandlung „Was ist Gerechtigkeit?" vorgebracht hat, lässt sich nicht mit Sicherheit sagen. Eher unwahrscheinlich erscheint es aber, dass Kelsen aus Furcht vor einer Blamage seine Replik unveröffentlicht gelassen hat, zumal die Interpretation der geistesgeschichtlichen Quellen in Kelsens Replik allemal glaubwürdiger und solider ausfällt als in Voegelins „Neuer Wissenschaft der Politik".

Bei zwei Wissenschaftlern, die einmal in einem Lehrer-Schüler-Verhältnis zueinander standen, aber später unterschiedlichen wissenschaftlichen Lagern angehörten, stellt sich darüber hinaus die Frage nach der Motivation einer wechselseitigen Kritik. Indem Voegelin Kelsen einem Brief[26] daran erinnert, dass die besten Schüler diejenigen seien, die später eigene Wege gingen, deutet er an, dass die von Kelsen geäußerte Irritation über die „Neue Wissenschaft der Politik" damit zusammen hängen könnte, dass Kelsen seinem ehemaligen Schüler möglicherweise nicht zubilligen will, eigene Wege in der Wissenschaft zu gehen. Hinzu kommt, dass Voegelin Hans Kelsens „Reine Rechtslehre" in seinem Buch über den „Autoritären Staat" einer ziemlich scharfen Kritik unterzogen hatte[27] (nachdem er in früheren Schriften Kelsens Rechtslehre noch gegen Missverständnisse in Schutz genommen hatte[28]).

Ist Hans Kelsens Replik auf Voegelins „Neue Wissenschaft der Politik" am Ende also nur eine Retourkutsche, entsprungen der Verärgerung eines gestrengen Lehrers über seinen unbotmäßigen Zögling? Glücklicherweise gibt es ein sehr einfaches und jedem Leser von Kelsens Replik zugängliches Mittel um herauszufinden, ob Kelsens Schrift eher durch persönliche Ressentiments oder vornehmlich sachlich-wissenschaftlich motiviert ist: Es genügt, darauf zu achten, ob Kelsens Einwände gegen Voegelins Schrift ernstzunehmende Argumente enthalten, oder ob dies nicht der Fall ist. Enthält Kelsens Schrift überwiegend ernstzunehmende Argumente, die sich auch ein späterer Leser, der Kelsens mögliche persönliche Vorbehalte gegen Voege-

[26] Schreiben Voegelins an Kelsen vom 10. Februar 1954. Der Biefwechsel befindet sich im Hans Kelsen Institut in Wien.

[27] Vgl. Eric Voegelin: Der autoritäre Staat. Ein Versuch über das österreichische Staatsproblem, Springer, Wien / New York 1997 (zuerst 1936), S. 102-149. - Zur Kritik Voegelins an Kelsens Reiner Rechtslehre vgl. Dietmar Herz: Das Ideal einer objektiven Wissenschaft von Recht und Staat. Zu Eric Voegelins Kritik an Hans Kelsen, 2.Aufl., München 2002. Zum selben Thema außerdem: Robert Chr. van Ooyen: Der Staat der Moderne. Hans Kelsens Pluralismustheorie, Duncker & Humblot, Berlin 2003, S.223-242.

[28] Beispielsweise noch in der Rezension:„Die Verfassungslehre von Carl Schmitt", in: The Collected Works of Eric Voegelin. Volume 13. Selected Book Reviews (ed. and trans. by Jodi Cockerhill and Bary Cooper), University of Missouri Press, Columbia / London 2001, S. 42-66 (44-46). Die Rezension, in der sich Voegelin bereits dem Standpunkt von Carl Schmitt zuneigt, erschien zuerst in: Zeitschrift für Öffentliches Recht 11 (1931), S. 89-109.

lin nicht teilt, zu eigen machen könnte, dann darf man getrost unterstellen, dass die Replik in erster Linie sachlich-wissenschaftlich motiviert war. Zwar kann grundsätzlich auch eine rationale Argumentation höchst individuellen und sogar tief irrationalen Motiven entspringen, aber dies bleibt irrelevant, solange die Argumentation wohlbegründet und in sich schlüssig und damit wissenschaftlich verwertbar ist.

Unter diesem Gesichtspunkt bleibt festzuhalten, dass Kelsen in seiner Replik durchwegs überaus klar und sachbezogen argumentiert, selbst dort, wo er polemisiert. Einigermaßen polemisch gerät Hans Kelsen seine Replik zwar an vielen Stellen, aber das ist grundsätzlich legitim, besonders, wenn man berücksichtigt, welche Zumutungen intellektueller und moralischer Art Voegelins „Neue Wissenschaft der Politik" enthält. Immerhin rechnet Voegelin Positivisten wie Hans Kelsen einer vermeintlich neuerwachten „Gnosis" zu und damit einer Strömung, die er im gleichen Atemzug für gemeingefährlich erklärt. Dass er Hans Kelsen in einem Brief vom 10. Februar 1954 von dem Vorwurf „Gnostiker" zu sein ausdrücklich ausnimmt, ist zwar ohne Zweifel eine höfliche Geste, ändert aber nichts an der Pauschalität der Vorwürfe, die Voegelin in der „Neuen Wissenschaft der Politik" erhebt und auch in späteren Veröffentlichungen immer wieder bekräftigt.[29] Dementsprechend ist Voegelins Rede vom „destruktiven Positivismus" keineswegs bloß im Sinne der nüchternen Feststellung zu sehen, auf die sich Voegelin in demselben Schreiben herausredet, daß die positivistischen Philosophen die Metaphysik nun einmal ablehnen. Vielmehr schwingt bei Voegelins Angriffen auf den Positivismus immer der Vorwurf mit, dass der Positivismus die geistigen Grundlagen der politischen Ordnung untergräbt.

3.3 Zur Beurteilung von Kelsens Replik

Wie ist nun aber Kelsens Voegelin-Kritik inhaltlich zu beurteilen? Enthalten Hans Kelsens sehr kritische Ausführungen zu Voegelins „Neuer Wissenschaft der Politik" tatsächlich ernsthafte Argumente, oder hat Kelsen bloß Voegelins Denkweise nicht verstanden? Dies soll im folgenden hinsichtlich

[29] So beklagt Voegelin sich einmal sehr bitter darüber, dass der „Sozialeinfluss" der von ihm geschätzten Form von „Wissenschaft von Menschen in Gesellschaft und Geschichte noch sehr gering" sei, „übertäubt durch das Marktgeschrei der politischen Intellektuellen und ihres Anhangs in wohlbefestigten Positionen – akademischen, parteilichen, gewerkschaftlichen, verlegerischen, journalistischen und anderen gesellschaftlichen Bollwerken", um dann mit den Worten fortzufahren: "Es wird viel Zeit, Überredung, Arbeit und wahrscheinlich auch Anwendung von Gewalt brauchen, um diese zerstörenden Faktoren auch nur soweit zurückzudrängen, dass sie nicht noch mehr Unheil anrichten, als sie schon angerichtet haben." Zitat aus: Eric Voegelin: Der Gottesmord. Zur Genese und Gestalt der modernen politischen Gnosis. (Hrsg von Peter J. Opitz.), Fink Verlag, München 1999, S. 56.

der wichtigsten Streitpunkte untersucht werden.

3.3.1 Wertfreiheit und Wissenschaftsideal

Eine der grundlegendsten Differenzen zwischen Voegelin und Kelsen bricht bei der Beurteilung der Wertfreiheitsfrage auf. Gibt es einen wissenschaftlichen Weg zur Erkenntnis der richtigen moralischen Werte und kommt der Wissenschaft neben der Vermittlung theoretischen Wissens dementsprechend auch eine Aufgabe der Werterziehung zu, wie Voegelin dies fordert?[30] Oder existiert keine solche wissenschaftliche Methode objektiver und allgemein verbindlicher Werterkenntnis, so dass die Wissenschaft der Wertvermittlung nicht nur nicht dienen kann, sondern, um nicht durch Vorurteile moralischer Art behindert zu werden, auch möglichst wertfrei betrieben werden sollte? Letzteres ist die Ansicht, die Hans Kelsen vertritt.

Die Werturteilsfrage gehört wohl zu den am meisten diskutierten wissenschaftsphilosophischen Problemen, zumindest was die Geistes- und Gesellschaftswissenschaften angeht. Es würde zu weit führen, die überaus kontroverse Diskussion an dieser Stelle erneut aufzurollen und sämtliche Argumente für und wider abzuwägen.[31] Die wichtigsten Ergebnisse dieser Diskussion lassen sich (aus meiner Sicht) in folgenden Punkten zusammen fassen:

1. Es gibt kein wissenschaftliches Verfahren, um Wertfragen zu entscheiden. Alle bisherigen Versuche die Gültigkeit oder Ungültigkeit von moralischen Werten zwingend zu beweisen sind gescheitert. Werte lassen sich grundsätzlich nicht rational begründen.

2. Die Wahrheit oder Falschheit wissenschaftlicher Aussagen hängt aber auch nicht von der Zustimmung oder Ablehnung irgendwelcher Werte ab. Aussagen über Tatsachen oder (natur-)gesetzliche Zusammenhänge sind unabhängig von Aussagen über Werte. In diesem Sinne ist die Wissenschaft wertfrei. Zumindest kann sie es sein.

[30] Vgl. Eric Voegelin: The German University and the Order of German Society: A Reconsideration of the Nazi Era, in: The Collected Works of Eric Voegelin. Volume 12. Published Essays 1966-1985 (ed. by Ellis Sandoz), Louisiana State University Press, Baton Rouge and London 1999, S. 1-35 (S. 26).

[31] Fast alle wesentlichen Aspekte der Werturteilsfrage findet man schon bei Max Weber auseinandergelegt. Vgl. Max Weber: Der Sinn der „Wertfreiheit" der soziologischen und ökonomischen Wissenschaften, in: Max Weber: Gesammelte Aufsätze zur Wissenschaftslehre, Tübingen 1988, S. 489-540. Vgl. Max Weber: Die „Objektivität" sozialwissenschaftlicher und sozialpolitischer Erkenntnis, in: Weber, Gesammelte Aufsätze zur Wissenschaftslehre, a.a.O., S. 146-214. - Einen Überblick über die neuere Diskussion erlaubt der Sammelband: Hans Albert / Ernst Topitsch (Hrsg.): Werturteilsstreit, Darmstadt 1971. - In Bezug auf Voegelins „Neue Wissenschaft der Politik" wird diese Frage erörtert in: Eckhart Arnold: Die Bewusstseinsphilosophie Eric Voegelins (als Grundlage politischer Ordnung), Magisterarbeit Universität Bonn 2000, S. 10-15, im Internet unter: http://www.eckhartarnold.de/papers/voegelin/node5.html .

3. Ungeachtet der inhaltlichen Wertfreiheit der Wissenschaft kommt der Wissenschaft als Institution im gesellschaftlichen Kontext eine Vielzahl von – oft sehr ambivalenten – Wertbezügen zu. Die Fragen etwa, welche Wissenschaftszweige gefördert werden sollen, welche Folgen die Verbreitung bestimmter wissenschaftlicher Erkenntnisse hat, und zu welchen Zwecken wissenschaftliche Erkenntnisse eingesetzt werden dürfen, sind nicht nur stark wertbezogene sondern sogar eminent politische Fragen.

Der erste dieser Punkte wird freilich von Eric Voegelin auf das Entschiedenste bestritten, behauptet Voegelin doch, dass eine politische Ordnungswissenschaft, die auch die Erkenntnis von Werten umfasst, durchaus möglich sei, ja, dass es eine solche Wissenschaft im antiken Griechenland bei Platon und Aristoteles und im Mittelalter bei Thomas von Aquin auch schon gegeben hätte.[32] Aber Voegelins Behauptung ist falsch. Denn keiner dieser Philosophen hat eine brauchbare Methode gefunden, um moralische Werte wissenschaftlich, d.h. in einer intersubjektiv nachvollziehbaren und überprüfbaren Weise, zu begründen. Es handelt sich daher bloß um einen simplen Bluff, wenn Voegelin auf das vermeintliche Faktum einer normativen politischen Ordnungswissenschaft in der griechischen Antike und im vorreformatorischen Christentum verweist. In einem Brief an Hans Kelsen[33] räumt Voegelin auch ein, dass es „keine Wissenschaft [gibt], die einen nachhaltigen Begriff der Gerechtigkeit entwickeln könnte, der nach Verifikationsregeln einer immanenten Wissenschaft als gültig festgestellt werden könnte", und dass „keiner der großen Philosophen [..] je einen wahnsinnigen Versuch dieser Art unternommen [hat]."

Nur was haben die großen Philosophen, die Voegelin als Gewährsmänner herbeizieht, dann getan? Um Voegelins Standpunkt zu stützen, müsste es ihnen mindestens auf irgendeine Weise gelungen sein, sittliche Werte in einer intersubjektiv verbindlichen Weise so zu begründen, dass niemand mehr ernsthaft bestreiten könnte, zur Beachtung dieser Werte verpflichtet zu sein. Dies nun hätte Voegelin an einer Interpretation der großen Philosophen schlüssig darlegen müssen. Wie wenig ihm das jedoch gelingt, führt beispielhaft seine Aristoteles-Interpretation aus „Order and History" vor Augen[34]: Voegelin spricht hier in einer für ihn ungewöhnlich offenen Weise einen fundamentalen Einwand gegen Aristoteles' Versuch einer Begründung der Ethik an, den Einwand nämlich, dass es sich dabei bloß um eine persön-

[32] Vgl. Voegelin, The New Science of Politics, a.a.O., S. 20.

[33] Brief vom 7. März 1954. Der Briefwechsel liegt im Hans Kelsen Institut in Wien. Eine Kopie befindet sich im Eric Voegelin Archiv in München.

[34] Vgl. Eric Voegelin: Order and History. Volume Three. Plato and Aristotle, Louisiana State University Press, Louisiana 1957, S. 299-303.

liche Meinung, sprich um „das, was Du denkst" handelt.[35] Die Antwort, die Voegelin auf diesen möglichen Einwand bei Aristoteles findet, besteht darin, dass eine moralische Überzeugung eben dann maßgeblich sei, wenn sie von einem „maßgeblichen Menschen" geäußert wird.[36] Doch damit wird das Problem offensichtlich nur verschoben. Auf die Frage, wonach bestimmt wird, wer als „maßgeblicher Mensch" gelten darf, geht Voegelin in der Folge gar nicht weiter ein. Vielmehr stimmt Voegelin nun ein Loblied darauf an, was für einen bedeutsamen Beitrag Aristoteles zur Erkenntnistheorie der Ethik doch geleistet hätte.[37] Anstatt also zu zeigen, wie Aristoteles das Begründungsproblem der Ethik löst, lobt Voegelin ihn dafür, dass er es auf eine so glänzende Weise getan hätte. Die Widerlegung des von ihm selbst zuvor aufgeworfenen Einwandes bleibt Voegelin dabei schuldig.

In dem bereits zitierten Brief an Hans Kelsen vom 7. März 1954 gibt Voegelin im Grunde auch zu, dass es keine wissenschaftliche Methode der Wertbegründung gibt, denn Voegelin beruft sich hier auf die Entstehung von Werten in den „Seelen der großen Propheten, Nomotheten, Philosophen und Heiligen". Damit ist aber nur eine – und nicht einmal eine besonders überzeugende – Antwort auf die empirische Frage gegeben, wie Werte entstehen. Der Hinweis darauf, wie bestimmte moralische Werte entstanden sind, oder wie moralische Werte überhaupt zu entstehen pflegen, stellt noch längst keine Begründung der Gültigkeit dieser Werte dar. Wesentliche Argumente, mit denen man den ersten der oben angeführten Punkte angreifen könnte, liefert Voegelins normative Ontologie nicht.

Nachdem dies geklärt ist, kann die Frage untersucht werden, wie vor dem Hintergrund der oben angeführten Resultate des Werturteilsstreits die unterschiedlichen Standpunkte zu beurteilen sind, die Eric Voegelin in der „Neuen Wissenschaft" der Politik und Hans Kelsen in seiner Replik zum Werturteilsstreit einnehmen. In dieser Frage ist Hans Kelsen grundsätzlich Recht zu geben, wenn er im Einklang mit Max Weber (den er sehr zu Recht gegen Voegelins plumpe Unterstellung, Weber habe an der Wertfreiheit nur festhalten können, weil er die Philosophie der Antike und des christlichen Mittelalters ignoriert habe, in Schutz nimmt) die Wertfreiheit der Wissenschaft einfordert. Ebenso kann man Hans Kelsens Feststellung zustimmen, dass die Vermittlung eines objektiven und damit wertfreien Wissens der politischen Realität an die Studenten der Politischen Wissenschaft ein „höchst sinnvolles" Unterfangen darstellt, „gerade weil sie die Wahl der Werte den Studenten selbst überlässt", und sie sich dadurch „der Tatsache bewusst werden, dass sie diese Wahl auf ihre eigene Verwantwortung treffen müssen."

[35]Ebda., S. 299.
[36]Vgl. ebda., S. 300.
[37]Vgl. ebda., S. 300.

Auf der anderen Seite muss jedoch eingeräumt werden, dass eine strikte Trennung von Werten und Tatsachen sich in der Praxis gerade in den Gesellschaftswissenschaften nur sehr schwer durchhalten lässt. Manchmal drängen sich bestimmte Wertfragen geradezu auf, z.B. beim wissenschaftlichen Vergleich unterschiedlicher politischer Systeme. Auch könnte man angesichts des dritten oben angeführten Punktes, der gesellschaftlichen Rolle der Wissenschaft als Institution, geradezu fordern, dass die damit verbundenen Verantwortungsfragen auch innerhalb der wissenschaftlichen Institutionen thematisiert werden. Es erschiene daher etwas artifiziell, wollte man die Erörterung jeglicher Wertfragen um jeden Preis aus den wissenschaftlichen Insitutionen verbannen.[38] Zudem muss man sich vor dem naiven Glauben hüten, weil irgendwelche Ansichten wissenschaftlich begründet sind, wären sie auch wertfrei, denn tatsächlich wird das Ideal der Wertfreiheit in der Wissenschaft oft nicht erfüllt.

Eines muss jedoch bei der Diskussion von Wertfragen im wissenschaftlichen Zusammenhang beachtet werden: Sofern Wertfragen erörtert werden oder innerhalb einer wissenschaftlichen Diskussion berührt werden, kann niemand eine wie auch immer geartete Fachautorität dafür in Anspruch nehmen. Es käme vielmehr einem Missbrauch der Fachautorität gleich, wenn – wie Voegelin sich dies vorzustellen scheint – von Hochschullehrern der Anspruch erhoben wird, an ihren Studenten Werterziehung zu leisten oder gar ihre Seelen zu formen.

3.3.2 Kelsens Analyse von Voegelins Repräsentationsbegriff

Ursprünglich sollte der Titel von Voegelins Werk nicht „Die Neue Wissenschaft der Politik“ sondern „Wahrheit und Representation“ lauten.[39] Der Repräsentationsbegriff ist denn auch eines der zentralen Themen der „Neuen Wissenschaft der Politik“. Freilich weicht Voegelins Begriff der Repräsentation vollkommen von dem im Staatsrecht und in der Politischen Wissenschaft etablierten Begriff der Repräsentation ab. Hinzu kommt, dass Voegelins Erörterung des Repräsentationsbegriffes keineswegs durch Klarheit glänzt. Die Schwierigkeiten, denen man begegnet, wenn man die Unklarheiten von Voegelins Repräsentationsbegriff entwirren und die Verwechselung mit dem herkömmlichen Begriff der Repräsentation vermeiden will, spiegeln sich auch in Hans Kelsens Replik wieder. Häufige Wiederholungen und Ein-

---

[38] Max Weber hat dies freilich mit gar nicht schlechten Argumenten gefordert. Ein Professor, so sah es Max Weber, sollte schließlich nicht den Katheder zur Verbreitung seiner politischen Ansichten nutzen, sondern er kann dies – genauso wie jeder andere Bürger auch – nach Feierabend im politischen Klub tun.

[39] Siehe das Vorwort von Dante Germino in Eric Voegelin: The New Science of Politics, a.a.O., S. V.

schübe, in denen Hans Kelsen immer wieder erklären muss, von welchem Repräsentationsbegriff gerade die Rede ist, deuten auf die Mühen hin, die ihm eine klare Analyse von Voegelins Repräsentationsbegriff bereitete.

Trotzdem gelingt es Hans Kelsen in bestechender Weise, die begriffliche Verwirrung aufzulösen, und dabei nicht nur die herkömmlichen Repräsentationsbegriffe von Voegelins Verständnis von Repräsentation sauber abzugrenzen, sondern auch Voegelins Repräsentationstheorie, soweit dies möglich ist, in klare Worte zu fassen. Nach dieser Klärung stellt sich die Lage ungefähr folgendermaßen dar:

Üblicherweise sind in den politischen Wissenschaften und im Staatsrecht zwei unterschiedliche Repräsentationsbegriffe geläufig: Erstens der Begriff der *Organrepräsentation*. Nach diesem Begriff ist z.B. ein Staatsoberhaupt ein Repräsentant seines Staates, wenn es rechtlich wie faktisch in der Lage ist, für diesen Staat selbstständig zu handeln und Entscheidungen zu treffen, die dann dem Staat als Ganzes zugeschrieben werden. (Ein spezifisch politischer Begriff der Repräsentation kann dabei von anderen Formen der Organrepräsentation gegebenenfalls dadurch abgegrenzt werden, dass im politischen Repräsentationsverhältnis der Handlungsbereich des Repräsentanten, also der Regierung des Staates, nicht von vornherein umgrenzt ist.) Die zweite Bedeutung des Wortes „Repräsentation" ist die der *demokratischen Repräsentation*. Eine Regierung ist repräsentativ, wenn sie demokratisch gewählt wurde. Auch wenn dasselbe Wort verwendet wird, beschreiben beide Begriffe unterschiedliche Dinge.

Demgegenüber gibt es bei Eric Voegelin drei unterschiedliche Repräsentationsbegriffe, die sich mit den üblichen Repräsentationsbegriffen nur ganz am Rande überschneiden, im Wesentlichen aber auf andere Fragen gemünzt sind: Der erste dieser Begriffe ist der Begriff der *deskriptiven Repräsentation*, worunter Voegelin in etwa die formellen Vorgänge, mit denen eine Regierung eingesetzt wird, zu verstehen scheint.[40] Voegelins Begriff der „deskriptiven Repräsentation" ist damit sehr viel weiter gefasst als der herkömmliche Begriff der demokratischen Repräsentation. Denn auch wenn sich Voegelins Beispiele vor allem auf Vorgänge innerhalb einer Demokratie (nämlich das Wahlverfahren) beziehen, könnte der Begriff ebensogut auf eine Diktatur bezogen werden, in der sich der Herrscher ganz einfach ausrufen lässt. Dadurch dass der Begriff der deskriptiven Repräsentation sehr viel weiter gefasst ist als der der demokratischen Repräsentation, unter den nur ein bestimmtes, nämlich das demokratische Einsetzungsverfahren fällt, bleibt er zugleich auch sehr viel gehaltloser. Es ist daher fraglich, warum Voegelin diesen Begriff überhaupt einführt, wenn er doch für die Sache, die er damit beschreiben möchte, ebenso treffend und zugleich sehr viel klarer z.B. vom

[40] Vgl. Voegelin, New Science of Politics, a.a.O., S. 32.

„Einsetzungsverfahren der Regierung" hätte sprechen können.

Der zweite von Voegelins Repräsentationsbegriffen beschreibt ein ganz anderes Problem, nämlich das Problem der Effektivität bzw. machtpolitischen Durchsetzungsfähigkeit einer Regierung oder eines Regimes oder eines politischen Systems.[41] Auch hier ist die Wortwahl Voegelins alles andere als einleuchtend, denn den Ausdruck *existentielle Repräsentation* wird ohne Erklärung niemand verstehen, während sofort verständlich wird, was gemeint ist, wenn z.B. von der „Fähigkeit zum Herrschaftserhalt" gesprochen wird. Voegelin scheint diesen Begriff nur einzuführen, um leichter gegen die demokratische Repräsentation polemisieren zu können. Dabei geht seine Polemik, wie Hans Kelsen sehr treffend herausstellt, jedoch vollkommen fehl, indem Voegelin den Theoretikern der Demokratie die Vernachlässigung eines Aspektes vorwirft, den sie durchaus nicht vernachlässigt haben, sondern nur unter einem anderen Titel als gerade dem der „Repräsentation" zu erörtern pflegen.[42]

Die dritte Stufe von Voegelins Repräsentationsbegriff, der Begriff der *Wahrheitsrepräsentation*, beschreibt wiederum einen vollkommen anderen Aspekt, nämlich den der religiösen Legitimation einer Herrschaft.[43] Voegelins Begriff der „Wahrheitsrepräsentation" ist nicht zuletzt deshalb so fragwürdig, weil Voegelin glaubt, dass die religiöse Legitimation einer Herrschaft tatsächlich mehr oder weniger wahr sein könnte. Dies musste Hans Kelsen geradezu absurd erscheinen, denn jede bekannte Religion stützt sich in irgendeiner Form auf ein metaphysisches Weltbild, dessen Wahrheit unmöglich erwiesen werden kann. Dementsprechend kann die religiöse Legitimation einer Herrschaft niemals eine andere Funktion haben als die einer Herrschaftsideologie. Wenn Voegelin nun nicht nur behauptet, dass eine religiöse Herrschaftslegitimation mehr oder weniger wahr sein könne, sondern geradezu fordert, dass die politische Ordnung sich auf die richtigen Tran-

[41]Vgl. Voegelin, New Science of Politics, a.a.O., S. 36ff.

[42]Claus Heimes verdanke ich den Hinweis, dass Voegelins Repräsentationsverständnis unmittelbar von Carl Schmitt beeinflusst sein könnte. Vgl. dazu Carl Schmitt: Verfassungslehre, 3. Aufl., Duncker und Humblot, Berlin 1957 (zuerst München und Leipzig 1928), S. 204-220. – In der Tat lehnt sich Voegelins Begriff der „existentiellen Repräsentation" an den Repräsentationsbegriff Carl Schmitts an, denn auch Carl Schmitt versteht Repräsentation ausdrücklich nicht als normativen Vorgang sondern als etwas „Existentielles", was Carl Schmitt folgendermaßen erläutert: „Die Idee der Repräsentation beruht darauf, dass ein als politische Einheit existierendes Volk gegenüber dem natürlichen Dasein einer irgendwie zusammenlebenden Menschengruppe eine höhere und gesteigerte, intensivere Art Sein hat." (ebd., S. 210.) An diese Art der „Daseinssteigerung" klingt Voegelins im Zusammenhang mit seiner Repräsentationstheorie entwickeltes Konzept der politischen „Artikulation" einer Gesellschaft zu einer historisch handlungsfähigen Einheit durch Bildung eines effektiven Herrschaftsverbands (sprich „existentielle Repräsentation") an.

[43]Vgl. Voegelin, New Science of Politics, S. 52ff.

szendenzerfahrungen gründen sollte, dann ist der Ideologieverdacht allerdings unausweichlich. Dies gilt umso mehr als Voegelin sich kaum der Mühe unterzieht, zu erklären, warum Herrschaft unbedingt religiös legitimiert werden muss. Ist eine in der richtigen Weise religiös legitimierte Herrschaft gerechter? Ist sie stabiler? Der Richtung von Voegelins Polemik nach zu urteilen, scheint Voegelin zu glauben, dass ohne die richtige religiöse Legitimation der Absturz in den Totalitarismus droht. Aber Voegelin unternimmt nicht den geringsten Versuch, diese Annahme auch nur ansatzweise empirisch zu untermauern.

Zweifellos hat Kelsen also die Schwachpunkte von Voegelins Repräsentationsbegriff richtig identifiziert. Kurz gefasst besagen Voegelins Ausführungen zu diesem Thema nämlich kaum mehr, als dass für ihn die Fragen, ob die Herrscher in der richtigen Weise regligös erleuchtet sind, und ob sie in der Lage sind sich durchzusetzen, eben sehr viel wichtiger sind, als die Frage, ob die Regierung demokratisch gewählt wird oder nicht. Der wissenschaftliche Wert von Voegelins Repräsentationsbegriff bleibt demgegenüber eher zweifelhaft.

3.3.3 Exkurs zu Voegelins Theorie der Wahrheitsrepräsentation: Voegelin als Theoretiker eines Mullah-Staates

Eine wichtige Frage, die sich vermutlich jedem Leser von Voegelins im engeren Sinne politiktheoretischen Schriften[44] stellt, die aber in der Sekundärliteratur zu Voegelin bisher noch kaum gestellt, geschweige denn ausführlich untersucht worden ist, ist die, welche Gestalt eine politisch Ordnung haben müsste, die den Maßstäben von Voegelins politischer Theorie entspricht. Die Beantwortung dieser Frage ist aber für die Beurteilung von Voegelins politischer Theorie von wesentlicher Bedeutung, denn ohne eine Antwort auf diese Frage erscheint eine angemessene Beurteilung von Voegelins politischem Denken, zu dessen religiösen Grundlagen man natürlich sehr unterschiedlich stehen kann, kaum möglich. Daher soll an dieser Stelle einmal versucht werden, wenigstens skizzenhaft eine Antwort auf diese Frage zu geben.[45]

---

[44] Neben der „Neuen Wissenschaft der Politik" wäre hier vor allem die Abhandlung „Was ist politische Realität?" in Voegelins bewusstseinsphilosophischen Werk „Anamnesis" zu nennen.

[45] Der mögliche Einwand, dass Voegelin nur als politischer Philosoph und Betrachter von höherer Warte aus gesprochen habe und daher nicht auf bestimmte Positionen hinsichtlich staatsorganisatorischer oder verfassungspolitischer Detailfragen festgelegt werden dürfe, geht aus zwei Gründen fehl: Zum einen hat sich Voegelin immer wieder auch zu tagespolitischen Fragen geäußert und dabei meist entschieden Stellung bezogen, wobei er seine Ansichten regelmäßig im Rückgriff auf seine politotheologischen Grundüberzeugungen rechtfertigte. Offenbar war es ihm also sehr wohl möglich aus seiner politischen Philosophie konkrete und greifbare politische Schlussfolgerungen zu ziehen. Zum anderen gibt es überhaupt nur zwei Möglichkeiten: Entweder lassen sich aus Voegelins politischer Philosophie irgendwelche Konsequenzen hinsichtlich

Als Vorgehensweise bietet es sich an, sich zunächst die zentralen Grundsätze von Voegelins politischer Theorie zu vergegenwärtigen, um dann nach einer Verfassung zu suchen, die diese Grundsätze möglichst weitgehend erfüllt.

Im Zentrum von Voegelins politischer Theorie steht der Grundsatz, dass die politische Ordnung sich auf eine – um Voegelins Jargon zu verwenden – deformationsfreie Erfahrung der Transzendenz stützen muss. Ohne diese Verankerung in der Transzendenz, die durch spirituell entsprechend sensible Individuen vermittelt werden muss, ist eine politische Ordnung für Voegelin nicht akzeptabel, ja beinahe nicht einmal denkbar. Die äußerste Gefahr für ein Gemeinwesen geht vom Abhandenkommen oder von der Verfälschung dieses Transzendenzbezuges aus. Konsequenterweise hat Voegelin daher auch einmal die Forderung aufgestellt, dass gegen Parteien „antichristlicher oder antiphilosophischer Art“ sehr entschieden mit Parteiverboten durchgegriffen werden müsse.[46]

Wie müsste nun die institutionelle Ordnung eines Systems beschaffen sein, das dem zentralen Grundsatz von Voegelins politischer Theorie Genüge leistet? In der Tat existiert ein politisches System, dass Voegelins Maßstäben in beinahe optimaler Weise gerecht wird. Es handelt sich dabei um das politische System der Islamischen Republik Iran. Die „Islamische Rpublik Iran“ trägt den Namen Republik nicht gänzlich zu unrecht. In diesem Land gibt es einige leidlich demokratische Institutionen: ein Parlament, eine gewählte Regierung, freie Wahlen, die offenbar auch nur in Grenzen (etwa durch den vorherigen Auschluss von Kandidaten) manipuliert werden. Aber über diesen Institutionen trohnt als oberstes Verfassungsorgan der „Religiöse Führer“, durch dessen Amt die Bewahrung der grundlegenden Prinzipien der politischen Ordnung des Iran sichergestellt wird. Unter diesen Prinzipien wird dabei in der Verfassung des Iran ausdrücklich der Glaube an die „Souveränität Gottes“, an die „göttliche Offenbarung“ und an die „Gerechtigkeit Gottes“ genannt.[47] Der Bezug zur Transzendenz – für Voegelin eine unerlässliche Grundvoraussetzung zumindest jeder guten politischen Ordnung – ist im Iran also bereits in der Verfassung fest verankert. In schönem Einklang mit Voegelins mehrstufiger Repräsentationslehre ist dabei der Transzendenz-

der Gestaltung von Politik und des Aufbaus der politischen Ordnung ziehen. Dann ist es aber auch legitim, danach zu fragen, worin diese Konsequenzen bestehen. Oder es lassen sich keinerlei institutionelle, verfassungsrechtliche oder allgemeinpolitische Konsequenzen aus Voegelins politischer Philosphie ziehen. Dann würde sich jedoch die Frage stellen, ob Voegelins Philosophie als politische Philosophie nicht überhaupt belanglos ist und sich in politischer Romantik und folgenlosem Mystizismus erschöpft.

[46] Vgl. Eric Voegelin: Die geistige und politische Zukunft der westlichen Welt (Vortrag vom 9. Juni 1959), München 1996, S. 33.

[47] Vgl. Artikel 2 der iranischen Verfassung. Quelle: Web-Projekt: International Constitutional Law auf: http://www.oefre.unibe.ch/law/icl/ir00000_.html

bezug dem demokratischen Prinzip eindeutig übergordnet, denn weder stehen die oben genannten Prinzipen zur Disposition demokratischer Entscheidungsprozeduren noch kann selbstverständlich der religiöse Führer demokratisch gewählt oder abgewählt werden.

Dem Religiösen Führer steht bei der Aufgabe der Bewahrung der islamischen Ordnung des Iran ein besonderes Verfassungsorgan, der sogenannte „Wächterrat", zur Seite. Dabei handelt es sich um ein zur Hälfte von Klerikern und zur Hälfte von Juristen gebildetes Gremium, dem die verantwortungsvolle Aufgabe obliegt sicherzustellen, dass die Grundsätze der islamischen Ordnung von Staat und Gesellschaft unangetastet bleiben.[48] Dazu verfügt der Wächterrat über außergewöhnliche Kompetenzen: So kann der Wächterrat beispielsweise nach gut dünken jeden Gesetzesentwurf zurückweisen, der nicht den Vorstellungen der klerikalen Mitglieder des Wächterrates über die richtige islamische Ordnung entspricht.[49] In Voegelins Terminologie könnte man dasselbe so formulieren: Dem Wächterrat obliegt die ehrenvolle Verpflichtung zu garantieren, dass die Gesetzgebung strikt im Sinne „adäquater Transzendenzerfahrungen" ausgeübt wird. Durch die Einrichtung des Wächterrates wird, wie man sieht, die zentrale Forderung von Voegelins politischer Theorie, dass die politische Ordnung auf eine gesunde Beziehung des Menschen zum transzendenten Seinsgrund aufbauen muss, in optimaler Weise verwirklicht. Dementsprechend erscheint die Bildung eines Wächterrates oder eines vergleichbaren Organs aus Voegelins Politikkonzeption heraus nicht nur folgerichtig, sondern geradezu geboten.

Alles in allem spricht also viel dafür, dass eine politische Ordnung wie die des Iran den politischen Vorstellungen Voegelins bestens entspricht, besser jedenfalls als die liberale Demokratie, bei der es doch stets dem Zufall überlassen bleibt, ob durch ihre Selektionsmechanismen ein Führungspersonal an die Macht gelangt, das über die nach Voegelins Ansicht für den Erhalt der politischen Ordnung unerlässlichen spirituellen Voraussetzungen verfügt.[50]

---

[48] Vgl. Artikel 91 der iranischen Verfassung. - Vgl. auch Vanessa Martin: Creating an Islamic State, I.B. Tauris Publishers, London / New York 2000, S. 162f.

[49] Vgl. Artikel 94 und Artikel 96 der Verfassung des Iran. - Den klerikalen Mitgliedern des Wächterrates kommt insofern ein Übergewicht zu, als sie über die Unvereinbarkeit von Gesetzen mit dem Islam allein, d.h. ohne die im Wächterrat vertretenen Juristen entscheiden, während umgekehrt über die Unverträglichkeit mit der Verfassung der Wächterrat in seiner Gesamtheit entscheidet.

[50] Dementsprechnd müsste die von Voegelins selbst einmal angedeutete Lösung des Problems mit Hilfe von vorwiegend in der politischen Kultur lokalisierten Stigmatisierungsmechanismen – das Amerika der McCarthy-Ära schwebte Voegelin dabei als Modell vor – mangels einer festen Institutionalisierung des alles entscheidenden religiösen Faktors noch als unzureichend beurteilt werden. Vgl. Eric Voegelin: Die Zukunft der westlichen Welt, a.a.O., S. 32-34.

3.3.4 Kelsen über die „Gnosistheorie“ und Voegelins Umgang mit der Geistesgeschichte

Ein nicht geringes Verdienst von Hans Kelsens Voegelin-Kritik besteht zweifellos darin, dass er Voegelins Interpretation der geistesgeschichtlichen Quellen sehr genau untersucht und dabei Voegelins nicht immer allzu gewissenhaften Umgang mit der Geistesgeschichte in einigen Fällen geradezu entlarvt. Besonders deutlich wird dies im Zusammenhang mit Voegelins „Gnosistheorie“, d.h. der Theorie, dass die große Mehrzahl der geistigen Strömungen der Moderne in ihrem Kern als gnostische Häresien zu verstehen seien, und dass daraus die Entstehung des Totalitarismus kommunistischer wie faschistischer Prägung hauptursächlich zu erklären sei.

Unter „Gnosis“ im engeren Sinne sind bestimmte, besonders im Frühchristentum auftretende, religiöse Strömungen zu verstehen, bei denen die dualistische Unterscheidung zwischen einem Reich des Lichtes und einem Reich der Finsternis besonders hervorgehoben wird, und die die Befreiung von der Finsternis durch ein geheimes, d.h. nicht offenbartes, mystisches Heilswissen lehren. Wird „Gnosis“ in diesem Sinne verstanden, so handelt es sich dabei um einen historischen Begriff, der einige örtlich und zeitlich einigermaßen genau lokalisierbare religiöse Strömungen beschreibt.

Der Begriff „Gnosis“ kann aber auch allgemeiner als Typenbegriff verstanden werden. Dann bezeichnet „Gnosis“ eine bestimmte religiöse Einstellung, deren wesentlichste Merkmale Dualismus und Erlösungsglaube sind. Voegelin verwendet den Begriff „Gnosis“ als Typenbegriff. Eine präzise Definition bleibt er jedoch schuldig. Voegelins Ausführungen in der „Neuen Wissenschaft der Politik“ kann man soweit entnehmen, dass für Voegelin das charakterisierende Merkmal der gnostischen Einstellung in dem Glauben besteht, das Reich Gottes ließe sich schon auf Erden verwirklichen.

In der „Neuen Wissenschaft der Politik“ argumentiert Eric Voegelin in zwei Richtungen: Zum einen versucht er eine neu-gnostische Traditionslinie aufzuweisen, die von ihrem ersten Erwachen in den Schriften eines gewissen Joachim Fiori im ausgehenden Mittelalter bis zum Nationalsozialismus reicht. Zum anderen bemüht sich Voegelin, in den Werken vermeintlich repräsentativer Vertreter einiger moderner politischer Bewegungen und Geistesströmungen gnostische Intentionen nachzuweisen.

Beides wird von Hans Kelsen vernichtend kritisiert. Sehr überzeugend weist Kelsen nach, dass die nationalsozialistische Ideologie und insbesondere das Symbol des „Dritten Reiches“ keineswegs auf Joachim Fiori zurückgeht, sondern sich – auch wenn es Analogien zwischen den Ideen des Joachim Fiori und der nationalsozialistischen Ideologie geben mag, und soweit man das überhaupt mit einiger Sicherheit sagen kann – im Wesentlichen aus einer anderen Quelle speist, nämlich aus Arthur Moeller van den Brucks

Dostojewski-Rezeption.

In diesem Zusammenhang entgeht Hans Kelsen natürlich auch nicht, wie wenig repräsentativ die geistesgeschichtlichen Belege sind, die Eric Voegelin auswählt. Voegelin nimmt diese Kritik in der „Neuen Wissenschaft der Politik" zwar vorweg und verteidigt sich damit, dass es ihm nicht um eine historische Darstellung sondern um die Analyse der „Struktur von gnostischen Erfahrungen und Ideen"[51] geht. Aber diese Verteidigung bleibt unzureichend, weil Voegelin gleichzeitig einen starken Kausalzusammenhang zwischen den „gnostischen Erfahrungen und Ideen" und der Entstehung verschiedener moderner politischer Bewegungen behauptet. Zum Nachweis dieses Kausalzusammenhanges hätte Voegelin aber repräsentative Vertreter der entsprechenden Bewegungen auswählen müssen.

Voegelins Ausführungen enthalten jedoch noch eine gravierendere Schwäche, die Hans Kelsen ebenfalls mit der Sorgfalt und Genauigkeit des Juristen aufdeckt: Voegelins Werkinterpretationen sind vom Hermeneutischen her oftmals unsauber. Besonders deutlich wird dies an Voegelins Vorwürfen gegen die Enzyklopädisten, denen er unterstellt, sie hätten mit ihrer *Ecyclopédie* einen „gnostischen Koran" aufstellen wollen, der alles andere Wissen verdrängen sollte. Dabei verkennt Voegelin in ziemlich mutwilliger Weise die ausdrücklich geäußerten Absichten der Enzyklopädisten, die in Wirklichkeit bloß ein Nachschlagewerk herausgeben wollten, um das Wissen ihrer Zeit möglichst weit zu verbreiten und jedem Interessierten zugänglich zu machen. Mit diesem Ziel verfolgten die Enzyklopädisten allerdings auch eine aufklärerische Absicht. Wenn Voegelin diese aufklärerische Absicht ablehnt, dann hätte er sie als solche kritisieren müssen, ohne den Enzyklopädisten unredliche Motive und verschwörerische Absichten zu unterstellen.

Ist Hans Kelsens Kritik von Voegelins „Gnosistheorie" bis zu diesem Punkt also in jeder Hinsicht Recht zu geben, so bleibt doch ein Aspekt von Voegelins „Gnosistheorie", in dem Kelsens Kritik etwas undifferenziert erscheint. Dieser Aspekt hängt mit Voegelins Interpretationsweise der philosophischen Klassiker zusammen. Voegelin verwendet eine Technik der psychologisch einfühlenden Interpretation, bei der weniger die Sachaussagen eines Denkers untersucht werden, sondern vielmehr dessen tiefere Motivation (in Voegelins Terminologie: die „seelischen Spannungen" bzw. die motivierenden geistigen „Erfahrungen") ergründet wird. Diese Technik ist natürlich sehr unsicher und kann, wie sich am Beispiel von Voegelins Interpretation der Motive der Enzyklopädisten gezeigt hat, leicht missbraucht werden. Dennoch ist diese Interpretationsweise nicht gänzlich illegitim, denn sie erlaubt es zuweilen aufschlussreiche Bezüge herzustellen. Insbesondere lassen

---

[51] Voegelin, The New Science of Politica, a.a.O., S. 151.

sich nachwirkende religiöse Überzeugungen oder auch einfach nur versteckte Vorurteile auf diese Weise aufdecken.

In einigen Fällen sind derartige religiöse Bezüge geradezu mit den Händen zu greifen. Dies ist ohne Zweifel bei dem französischen Positivisten Auguste Comte der Fall, der in seiner letzten Schaffensphase sogar die Gründung einer Positivstenkirche plante.[52] In einem anderen Fall, bei Karl Marx und Friedrich Engels, ist der eschatologische Zug ihrer historischen Theorie oft beschrieben worden.[53] Und zweifellos ist dieser eschatologische Zug auch eine sehr problematische und darum wichtige Eigenschaft dieser Theorie, denn unter anderem aus dem eschatologischen Geschichtsbild ließen sich später beinahe unbeschränkte Rechtfertigungslizenzen revolutionärer Gewalt ableiten. Insofern trifft Kelsen nur einen wenig entscheidenden Punkt, wenn er gegen Voegelin darauf beharrt, dass die Philosophien von Comte und Marx hochgradig rationale Philosophien seien. Schließlich können sich auch in eine rationale Philosophie oder in eine Philosophie im rationalistischen Jargon tief irrationale Züge einmischen.[54] Es kann sich daher sehr wohl lohnen, dem „Christentum im Atheismus" nachzuspüren.

Andererseits urteilt Voegelin, wenn er bei bestimmten Denkern verborgene gnostische Bezüge oder religiöse Bezüge anderer Art aufdeckt, zumeist sehr ungerecht. So erscheint es nicht recht verständlich, warum er einerseits Comte und Marx verwirft und auf der anderen Seite beispielsweise die Philosophie Platons oder auch das vorreformatorische Christentum als Alternativen von noch unverdorbener Glaubenswahrheit preist. Schließlich ist die politische Ordnung, die Platon im „Staat" entwirft, durchaus totalitär zu nennen. Doch während Voegelin den aufklärerischen und revolutionären Philosophen gar nicht genug Vorwürfe machen kann, sieht er über die problematischen Züge von Platons politischer Philosophie sehr großzügig hinweg. Vielleicht achtete er die Spiritualität von Platons Philosophie so hoch, dass er ihre fragwürdigen Seiten nicht mehr sehen wollte. Daran, dass eine spirituell niveauvolle Philosophie wie die Platons in politischer Hinsicht dennoch ziemlich verheerend ausfallen kann, zeigt sich aber nur noch einmal mehr, wie irrelvant der spirituelle Hintergrund für die Beurteilung politischer Theorien im Grunde ist.

Letzteres verweist auf eine weitere fundamentale Schwäche von Voegelins „Gnosistheorie", die Hans Kelsen schon gar nicht mehr anspricht: Selbst

---

[52] Vgl. Werner Fuchs-Heinritz: Auguste Comte, Westdeutscher Verlag, Opladen/Wiesbaden 1998, S. 235ff.

[53] Vgl. Leszek Kolakowski: Die Hauptströmungen des Marxismus. 1.Band, 2.überarbeitete Auflage, München 1981. - Leszek Kolakowski hält das „prophetische" Moment im Werk von Marx selbst – im Gegensatz zur späteren Wirkungsgeschichte – jedoch nicht für sehr dominant.

[54] Kelsen scheint dies später jedoch eingesehen zu haben. Vgl. Rudolf Aladár Métall: Hans Kelsen. Leben und Werk, Wien 1969, S. 91.

wenn es Voegelin gelungen wäre, schlüssig zu beweisen, dass der ganze von ihm aufgezählte Reigen moderner Denker und Geistesströmungen ein Ausdruck gnostischer Religiosität ist, dann bleibt immer noch die Frage offen, warum die „Gnosis" als politisch hochgefährliche religiöse Bewegung gefürchtet werden muss. Die Tatsachen sprechen hier keineswegs für sich, da nur einige wenige der von Voegelin als gnostisch charakterisierten politischen Bewegungen in eine totalitäre Herrschaft mündeten. Auch Voegelins ständig wiederholter Vorwurf, der Gnostizismus sei ein Ausdruck der Realitätsverweigerung, greift ins Leere, denn dies ist ein Vorwurf, den man mit Fug und Recht gegen jede religiöse Weltanschauung erheben kann. Aus dem Maß der Realitätsverweigerung kann man deshalb keine unmittelbaren Schlußfolgerungen hinsichtlich der politischen Gefährlichkeit einer religiösen Überzeugung ableiteten.

Zusammenfassend lässt sich sagen, dass Hans Kelsen sehr überzeugend nachweist, wie wenig Voegelins „Gnosistheorie" als wissenschaftliche Theorie ernst genommen werden kann. Es trifft den Kern der Sache, wenn Kelsen feststellt, dass das Wort „Gnosis" bei Voegelin den Charakter eines Schimpfwortes („invective") und nicht den eines präzisen wissenschaftlichen Begriffes hat. Man täte Voegelin auch keinen Gefallen damit, wollte man seine „Gnosistheorie" ernsthaft als wissenschaftliche Theorie gelten lassen, denn eine politikwissenschaftliche Theorie, die es nicht mehr erlaubt, zwischen einer liberaldemokratischen und einer totalitären Einstellung zu unterscheiden – eine Unterscheidung, die bei Voegelins unterschiedsloser Anwendung des Gnosisvorwurfes auf liberaldemokratische Politiker ebenso wie auf kommunistische Regime in den polemischen Schlusspassagen der „Neuen Wissenschaft der Politik" nicht mehr erkennbar ist –, wäre nichts weniger als eine intellektuelle Bankrotterklärung ihres Erfinders.

3.3.5 Abschließende Bemerkungen zu Voegelins politischer Theologie

Voegelins politisches Denken kann man als eine Form von Politischer Theologie auffassen. Politische Theologie ist Voegelins Philosophie vor allem in dem Sinne, dass Voegelin die politische Gesellschaft sowohl in der theoretischen Beschreibung als auch in der normativen Zielsetzung als religiöse Gemeinschaft versteht. Jede politische Ordnung beruht für Voegelin auf bestimmten religiösen „Erfahrungen", die, wenn sie von dem dafür kompetenten Fachpersonal, das sich aus Philosophen, Propheten, Aposteln, Nomotheten und dergleichen zusammensetzt, erfolgreich in die Gesellschaft hinein vermittelt werden, eine Gemeinschaft stiften, die durch eine bis tief in die Seelen der Einzelnen hinabreichende Verbindung der Gemeinschaftszugehörigen untereinander gekennzeichnet ist. Diese Vorstellung von politischer Ordnung bildet freilich eher eine Idealvorstellung Voegelins, die er im Einzelnen noch durch allerlei einschränkende Klauseln und realistische Anpassungen abschwächt.

Gegen Voegelins politische Theologie lassen sich zwei Arten von Einwänden formulieren, theologische und pragmatische. Die pragmatischen Einwände betreffen die Frage, ob Voegelins Idealbild von politischer Ordnung realistisch und daher als Leitfaden für die Gestaltung der Ordnung zu empfehlen ist, gesetzt man unterstützt die zu Grunde liegenden Werte. Die theologischen Einwände berühren dagegen das Problem, ob Voegelins Vorstellungen von der Transzendenz und der Seele angemessen und richtig sind.

Die Beurteilung theologischer Fragen hängt natürlich ganz und gar vom jeweiligen religiösen Standpunkt ab. Auch wenn es interessant wäre, einmal der Frage nachzugehen, inwiefern Voegelins mystische Religiösität mit dem Prinzip der Offenbarunsreligion vereinbar ist, nach dem die Offenbarung jedem glaubenswilligen Menschen zugänglich ist, und nicht bloß einer kleinen Elite seelisch besonders sensibler Individuen, sollen hier nur die pragmatischen Einwände erörtert werden.

Anders als die theologischen Einwände lassen sich die pragmatischen Einwände zumindest im Prinzip empirisch rechtfertigen. In pragmatischer Hinsicht ist gegen Voegelins politische Theologie einzuwenden, dass ihr vollkommen falsche Auffassungen darüber zugrunde liegen, was die Bedingungen guter politischer Ordnung sind (nach welchem Maßstab auch immer). Voegelin glaubt, gute politische Ordnung sei vor allem eine Frage der Spiritualität. Allerdings hat er, wie schon festgestellt, nirgendwo einen Nachweis dieses Kausalzusammenhangs geliefert. In Wirklichkeit ist die Güte der politischen Ordnung aber vor allem eine Frage des institutionellen Designs. Die Suche nach einem geeigneten Ensemble politischer Instiutionen, das es erstens erlaubt, überhaupt Ordnung zu stiften, und das sich zweitens selbst wiederum gegen Missbrauch absichert, ist ein langwieriger historischer Prozess, dessen Ergebnisse weit mehr auf Erfahrungswissen und Lebensweisheit beruhen als auf berechenbarer Wissenschaft. Man könnte in Anlehnung an Voegelins Terminologie sagen, dass sich im Laufe dieses Prozesses ein „Ordnungswissen" angesammelt hat, das Ordnungswissen der liberalen Demokratie nämlich, das uns lehrt, durch welche politischen Insitutionen die Rechte der Einzelnen geschützt werden können und zugleich ihre Freiheit gesichert werden kann.

Wenn sich eine politische Theorie wie die von Eric Voegelin durchsetzt, dann besteht die Gefahr, dass dieses Ordnungswissen erodiert, da ihm im Rahmen von Voegelins Ansatz keinerlei oder nur eine völlig untergeordnete Bedeutung beigemessen werden kann. Die Gefahr, die von Voegelins politischer Theorie dadurch ausgeht, ähnelt, wenn auch in abgeschwächtem Maße, der Gefahr, die dem politischen Denken von Karl Marx einwohnt. Marx sah im Staat bekanntlich einzig und allein ein Unterdrückungsinstrument der herrschenden Klasse. Ist die Klassenherrschaft erst einmal abgeschafft, dann, so glaubte Marx, würde auch der Staat absterben. Dementsprechend fehlen dem Marxismus weitgehend diejenigen Elemente politischer Theorie, die sich mit der Organisation und Zähmung der staatlichen Herrschaft beschäftigen. Nicht zuletzt auf diesen theoretischen Mangel dürfte es zurückzuführen sein, dass die meisten der sich auf den Marxismus stützenden Herrschaftsformen in die Diktatur abgeglitten sind. Man kann mutmaßen, dass ein Voegelianismus als politische Bewegung aus ähnlichen Gründen Gefahr liefe, in ein Mullah-Regime abzugleiten.

Abgesehen von den wissenschaftlichen Schwächen von Voegelins „Neuer Wissenschaft der Politik", die dank Hans Kelsens eingehender Kritik nunmehr hinreichend deutlich zu Tage getreten sein dürften, beruht Voegelins Politische Theologie – und wahrscheinlich auch jede andere Politische Theologie – auf einem grundlegenden Irrtum. Dieser Irrtum besteht in der Annahme, oder wie man vielleicht genauer sagen müsste, in der Erwartung, dass der Politik bzw. der politischen Ordnung auch eine spirituelle Funktion zukommen müsse. Aber diese Erwartung muss notwendig enttäuscht werden, denn in Wahrheit ist das Politische ein reiner Profanbereich des menschlichen Lebens. Die primäre Aufgabe der Politik besteht darin, die Menschen eines Landes unter einer Rechtsordnung zu vereinen und ihnen so ein friedliches Zusammenleben zu ermöglichen. Dies erfordert keineswegs die Stiftung einer quasi-religiösen Gemeinschaft bzw. von „Ordnung in Geschichte", wenn „Ordnug" mehr bedeuten soll als bloß Frieden und Gerechtigkeit in dem aller äußerlichsten und profansten Sinne. Kaum jemand hat das deutlicher gesehen als Hans Kelsen, für den die Zugehörigkeit zur politischen Gemeinschaft in seelischer Hinsicht wenig mehr darstellt als eine Art Vereinsmitgliedschaft. Spirituelle Führung oder einen Beitrag zum Sinn des Lebens kann man von der politschen Sphäre jedenfalls nicht erhoffen. Und das ist auch besser so.

3.4 Literatur

Albert, Hans / Topitsch, Ernst (Hrsg.): Werturteilsstreit, Darmstadt 1971.

Arnold, Eckhart: Eric Voegelins Bewußtseinsphilosophie (als Grundlage politischer Ordnung), Magisterarbeit, Universität Bonn 2000. (Im Internet unter: http://www.eckhartarnold.de/papers/voegelin/index.html (letzter Zugriff am 20.7.2004).)

Anderson, William: Review of Eric Voegelin: The New Science of Politics, in: The Journal of Politics, Official Organ of The Southern Political Science Association, Vol. 15, No. 4, pp. 563-568.

Baruzzi, Arno: Kritik der Moderne nach Voegelin und Heidegger. Thesen und Fragen, in: Zeitschrift für Politik, 2001, S. 257ff.

Bischof, Achim: Zur Biographie von Hans Kelsen, auf: www.hans-kelsen.de (letzter Zugriff 20.11.2003).

Buckley, F.R.: The Dreamers, Review of The New Science of Politics by Eric Voegelin, in: The Freeman, Vol. 5, No. 14 (August 1955), pp. 621-622.

Catlin, George: Review of Eric Voegelin: The New Science of Politics, in: Political Studies, Vol. 11, No. 2 (June 1954), pp. 174-175.

Cooper, Barry: Constituent elements in the genesis of Voegelin's political science, in: Zeitschrift für Politik, 2001, S. 243ff.

Dahl, Robert A.: The Science of Politics: New and Old (Review of David Easton: The Political System: An inquiry into the State of Political Science, New York 1953 and Eric Voegelin: The New Science of Politics: An Introductory Essay, Chicago 1952), in: World Politics, Vol. 7, No. 3 (April 1955), pp. 480-489.

Farrell, Thomas J.: The Key Question. A critique of professor Eugene Webbs recently published review essay on Michael Franz's work entitled "Eric Voegelin and the Politics of Spiritual Revolt: The Roots of Modern Ideology", in: Voegelin Research News, Volume III, No.2, April 1997, auf: http://vax2.concordia.ca/~vorenews/v-rnIII2.html (Host: Eric Voegelin Institute, Lousiana State University. Zugriff am: 17.11.2000).

Fuchs-Heinritz, Werner: Auguste Comte, Westdeutscher Verlag, Opladen/Wiesbaden 1998.

Hallowell, John H.: Review of Eric Voegelin: The New Science of Politics, in: Lousiana Law Review - Vol. XIII No. 3 (March 1953), pp. 525-530.

Henkel, Michael: Eric Voegelin zur Einführung, Junius Verlag, Hamburg 1998.

Herz, Dietmar: Das Ideal einer objektiven Wissenschaft von Recht und Staat. Zu Eric Voegelins Kritik an Hans Kelsen, 2. Aufl., München 2002.

Kelsen, Hans: Allgemeine Staatslehere, Springer Verlag, Berlin 1925.

Kelsen, Hans: Reine Rechtslehre, Wien 1992 (Nachdruck der zweiten Auflage von 1960).

Kelsen, Hans: Vom Wesen und Wert der Demokratie, 2.Neudruck der 2.Auflage (Tübingen 1929), Aalen, Scientia-Verlag, 1981.

Kolakowski, Leszek: Die Hauptströmungen des Marxismus. 1.Band, 2.überarbeitete Auflage, München 1981 (erste Auflage München 1977).

Lübbe, Hermann: Zustimmungsfähige Modernität. Gründe einer marginal verbliebenen Rezesption Eric Voegelins, München 2003.

Lübbe, Hermann: Säkularisierung. Geschichte eines ideenpolitischen Begriffs, München 1965.

Martin, Vanessa: Creating an Islamic State, I.B. Tauris Publishers, London / New York 2000.

Métall, Rudolf Aladár: Hans Kelsen. Leben und Werk, Deuticke Verlag, Wien 1969.

van Ooyen, Robert Chr.: Der Staat der Moderne. Hans Kelsens Pluralismustheorie, Duncker & Humblot, Berlin 2003.

van Ooyen, Robert Chr.: Totalitarismustheorie gegen Kelsen und Schmitt: Eric Voegelins „politische Religionen“ als Kritik an Rechtspositivismus und politischer Theologie, in: Zeitschrift für Politik, 2002, S. 56ff.

Poirier, Maben W.: VOEGELIN- - A Voice of the Cold War Era ...? A COMMENT on a Eugene Webb review, in: Voegelin Research News, Volume III, No.5, October 1997, auf: http://vax2.concordia.ca/˜vorenews/V-RNIII5.HTML (Host: Eric Voegelin Institute, Lousiana State University. Zugriff am: 17.11.2000).

Ranke, Joachim: Rezension von Eric Voegelins „Neuer Wissenschaft der Politik“ in: Zeitschrift für Staatswissenschaft 111/1, S. 173-179.

Schabert, Thilo: Die Werkstatt Eric Voegelins, in: Zeitschrift für Politik, 2002, S. 83ff.

Schmitt, Carl: Verfassungslehre, 3. Aufl., Duncker und Humblot, Berlin 1957 (zuerst München und Leipzig 1928).

Sontheimer, Kurt: Antidemokratisches Denken in der Weimarer Republik, dtv Wissenschaft, München 1983.

Voegelin, Eric: Anamnesis. Zur Theorie der Geschichte und Politik, München 1966.

Voegelin, Eric: Autobiographical Reflections (ed. by Ellis Sandoz), Louisiana State University Press, Baton Rouge and London 1996.

Voegelin, Eric: Die geistige und politische Zukunft der westlichen Welt (Vortrag vom 9.Juni 1959), München 1996.

Voegelin, Eric: Der Gottesmord. Zur Genese und Gestalt der modernen politischen Gnosis. (Hrsg von Peter J. Opitz.), Fink Verlag, München 1999.

Voegelin, Eric: Die Größe Max Webers (hrsg. v. Peter J. Opitz), München, Fink Verlag, 1995.

Voegelin, Eric: Ordnung und Geschichte. Band 7. Aristoteles. (Hrsg. von Peter J. Opitz, aus dem Englischen von Helmut Winterholler), Fink Verlag, München 2001 (englisches Original Baton Rogue 1957).

Voegelin, Eric: The New Science of Politics, An Introduction, Chicago/London 1987. (Zuerst erschienen: Chicago 1952; Deutsche Erstausgabe: Eric Voegelin: Die Neue Wissenschaft der Politik. Eine Einführung, München 1959.)

Voegelin, Eric: Der autoritäre Staat. Ein Versuch über das österreichische Staatsproblem, Springer, Wien / New York 1997 (zuerst 1936).

Voegelin, Eric: Die Verfassungslehre von Carl Schmitt, in: The Collected Works of Eric Voegelin. Volume 13. Selected Book Reviews (ed. and trans. by Jodi Cockerhill and Bary Cooper), University of Missouri Press, Columbia / London 2001, S. 42-66. Zuerst erschienen in: Zeitschrift für Öffentliches Recht 11 (1931), S. 89-109.

Voegelin, Eric: Die geistige und politische Zukunft der westlichen Welt. (Hrsg. von Peter J. Opitz und Dietmar Herz), München 1996.

Weber, Max: Gesammelte Aufsätze zur Wissenschaftslehre. (Hrsg. von Johannes Winckelmann), Tübingen 1988.

Briefwechsel zwischen Hans Kelsen und Eric Voegelin mit Briefen vom 26. Januar 1954 (Kelsen an Voegelin), 10. Februar 1954 (Voegelin an Kelsen), 27. Februar 1954 (Kelsen an Voegelin), 7. März 1954 (Voegelin an Kelsen),

27. Juli 1954 (Kelsen an Voegelin). Der Briefwechsel liegt im Hans Kelsen-Institut in Wien. Eine Kopie des Briefwechsels befindet sich im Eric Voegelin Archiv in München.

Constitution of the Islamic Republic of Iran, auf: http://www.oefre.unibe.ch/law/icl/ir00000_.html